THE RIXI ♥ MARKUS
BOOK OF BRIDGE

WILLOW BOOKS
Collins
8 Grafton Street
London W1
1985

Willow Books
William Collins Sons & Co Ltd
London · Glasgow · Sydney
Auckland · Toronto · Johannesburg

First published 1985
© Rixi Markus 1985

Markus, Rixi
The Rixi Markus Book of Bridge
1. Contract bridge
I. Title
795.41′5   GV1282.3

ISBN 0 00 218167 3

Filmset in Great Britain by
Rowland Phototypesetting Ltd, Bury St Edmunds, Suffolk
Printed and bound in Great Britain by
Robert Hartnoll, Bodmin

CONTENTS

FORWORD

At last *The Rixi Markus Book of Bridge*, containing a selection of the best hands from my *Guardian* bridge column, is being published in the year in which I celebrate 30 years as the weekly bridge correspondent of the *Manchester Guardian* and the *Weekly Guardian*. It has been a great privilege to write for *The Guardian* especially as I am the only woman bridge correspondent in Britain and I would like to thank my readers for their wonderful support and encouraging letters which have made my task much easier and more enjoyable. My main ambition as a writer has always been not to bore my readers but to make them eager to read all.

I think this book contains something for most players. I have included material from the past to prove that bridge has been played at the highest level for a very long time and though systems, gadgets and many other complicated methods have now taken over, the main essence of the game – playing and defending contracts – requires the same ingredients as before. The old masters knew all the answers even if our present champions often believe that they have just discovered the secret of success at the table. Bridge is a wonderful game and I hope it will remain so and that common sense will prevail over distorted ideas; logic and common sense are still the best guidelines for any type of player.

I must acknowledge that I could hardly have produced this book without the assistance of Eric Crowhurst who helped me select the material, arrange the various chapters and correct some errors. He was also responsible for the typing of the manuscript and the proofreading. In fact he did most of the hard work for which I owe him my gratitude and appreciation. After writing a book, it becomes difficult to notice mistakes when looking at it again but it is obviously important that there should be none for the reader – so again my thanks to Eric.

R.M.

BIDDING

I   Doing What Comes Naturally

For one reason or another, I have not played with a regular partner in this country for the last few years. However, I have been fortunate enough to play in tournaments all over the world with a number of world-famous and brilliant partners like Giorgio Belladonna, Pietro Forquet, Zia Mahmoud, Benito Garozzo, Leon Tintner, Karl Rohan and many others. As you can imagine, these players are all used to playing extremely complex bidding systems with their more regular partners, but I am always able to persuade them to adopt my own natural style of bidding when they are playing with me: a strong no trump, Stayman, Blackwood and possibly one or two gadgets like Jacoby Transfers. In my view, the remarkable thing about these arrangements is that we always get on so well, despite the fact that my illustrious partners are playing a bidding system with which they are quite unfamiliar. We have very few bidding misunderstandings, and there are very few hands on which we have cause to regret the lack of more sophisticated bidding methods.

One might expect that it would be in the slam zone where unaccustomed partnerships would feel the lack of a comprehensive bidding system. In practice, however, I believe that good judgement at high levels is far more important than a long list of specialised conventions, and I have found that my irregular partners and I manage to cope remarkably well on the slam hands which come our way. Here are a few examples of our simple methods in action.

HAND 1 This is from the 1983 Guardian Easter Tournament, where I won the three-session Pairs Championship with the Pakistani star, Zia Mahmoud.

	West		*East*
♠	A K Q J 7 2	♠	10 3
♡	9 8 3	♡	A K Q J 2
◇	Q 7	◇	A 6 3
♣	Q 10	♣	A 9 6

West	*East*
Mahmoud	Mrs Markus
1♠	3♡
4♠(1)	4NT
5◇	5NT
6◇	7NT
NB	

(1) Showing a solid six-card or longer suit.

South led a passive spade against 7NT. I won in the closed hand with the 10 and tested the heart suit. South showed out on the first round, but I was able to cross to dummy with a spade and run the 9 of hearts to pick up North's exposed 10 and make all 13 tricks.

HAND 2 This occurred in the Mixed Pairs Championship at the 1983 International Bridge Festival in Deauville. I was playing with the British international player, Willie Coyle, for the first time.

West	*East*
♠ A Q 10 9	♠ K J
♡ A 8	♡ K Q J 9 2
◇ A Q J 9 8	◇ 7 4
♣ 8 3	♣ A K 10 4

West	*East*
Mrs Markus	Coyle
1♠(1)	3♡
4NT	5◇
5NT(2)	7♡(3)
NB	

(1) I always prefer to open with a major suit in a pairs event, provided that I have a convenient rebid available over any possible response.

(2) Asking for kings and, most important, guaranteeing that the partnership held all four aces.

(3) This knowledge enabled my partner to bid seven on the strength of his solid heart suit and vital black kings.

There was no problem in the play of seven hearts: a club ruff in dummy provided the vital 13th trick.

HAND 3 Strangely, this hand occurred during the same event as Hand 2.

	West	East
♠	A K 9 2	Q 4
♡	8 7 6	A K Q 10 2
◇	Q 4	A K 7
♣	K J 7 3	A 8 4

West	East
Mrs Markus	Coyle
1♠(1)	3♡
4♡	4NT(2)
5◇	5NT
6♡	7NT
NB	

(1) Once again getting the major suit in first. Playing a strong no trump throughout in the CAB style, a rebid of 2NT over a response at the two-level shows a minimum opening hand.

(2) The raise to four hearts meant that my partner could now count five heart tricks, and he also knew that the queen of spades was likely to be a vital card.

Those are just three examples of the effectiveness of simple, natural methods on big hands. If space permitted, I could quote scores of other examples with the same theme, and my experience of playing with a great many different partners in a great many different countries confirms what I have always maintained: that one does not need a complex bidding system in order to cope perfectly satisfactorily with the vast majority of hands; in the main, common sense, good judgement and, on occasions, a little bit of luck will work just as effectively. To my mind, there are five major advantages to be gained by bidding in a basically natural, Acol style:

(*a*) It enables you to play with any number of different partners without needing to hold a committee meeting first in order to devise your bidding system.

(*b*) It conveys less information to the opponents, who, it must be remembered, will probably end up defending against your final contract. Complex question-and-answer auctions can be quite helpful in setting the best contract, but they also help the opponents to find the best defence.

(*c*) It makes the game much simpler from the point of view of the spectator. Bridge, like all other sports, needs sponsors; sponsors need spectators in order to make their advertising effective; spectators need to be able to understand what is going on; and spectators will not know what is going on if the bidding is nothing more than an unintelligible codified exchange of information.

(*d*) On a great many hands, what I call natural bidding actually works better than artificial methods. This is particularly true when the opponents intervene and the auction becomes competitive, but it can also apply in uncontested sequences. Here is a typical example from the 1984 World Team Olympiad in Seattle, where I watched a top Canadian pair struggling with what seemed to me to be an extremely straightforward hand.

West	*East*
♠ Q 3	♠ A J 7 6 5 4 2
♡ K 7 3	♡ 10 4
♢ A K J 9 5	♢ Q 8 6
♣ K Q 10	♣ J

You and I would probably bid 1♢–1♠–2NT–4♠, or possibly 1NT–2♡(transfer)–2♠–4♠. This was the Canadian auction:

West	*East*
1♢	1♠
2NT	3♣
3♢	3♠
3NT	4♣
4♢	4♠
4NT	5♠
NB	

With the ace of hearts favourably placed, declarer had to avoid a trump loser in order to make his perilous contract of five spades. He managed this by leading the 3 of spades from dummy and collecting the singleton king from North, but he may not be so lucky next time.

(*e*) It makes the game so much easier for the players themselves. The strain of memorising page after page of conventions is certain to tell in a long event like the World or European Championship, and players who do not have to struggle with complex conventional sequences on nearly every hand must be in better shape to solve the many problems which occur in the play and defence.

My personal view is that this factor almost certainly cost the Italians the 1983 Bermuda Bowl World Championship. After a marvellously close match against North America, in which the lead changed hands on no fewer than 22 occasions during the 176 boards, the Italians led by 8 imp with just two boards remaining. This was the crucial penultimate board.

Dealer East; East–West vulnerable.

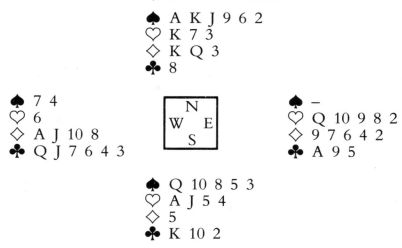

```
                ♠ A K J 9 6 2
                ♡ K 7 3
                ♢ K Q 3
                ♣ 8

   ♠ 7 4              N              ♠ —
   ♡ 6          W          E         ♡ Q 10 9 8 2
   ♢ A J 10 8         S              ♢ 9 7 6 4 2
   ♣ Q J 7 6 4 3                     ♣ A 9 5

                ♠ Q 10 8 5 3
                ♡ A J 5 4
                ♢ 5
                ♣ K 10 2
```

When the US team held the North–South cards, the bidding was as follows:

South	West	North	East
Hamman		Wolff	
			NB
1♠	NB	4NT	NB
5♢	NB	5♠	NB
NB	NB		

With the adverse cards lying quite favourably, South made 11 tricks in some comfort.

At the other table:

South	West	North	East
Garozzo		Belladonna	
			NB
1♠	NB	2NT(1)	NB
3♣(2)	NB	4NT(3)	NB
5◇(4)	NB	6♠	NB
NB	NB		

(1) In the Italian system, this showed a strong hand with spade support and a singleton or void elsewhere.

(2) Showing a minimum or sub-minimum opening bid.

(3) At this point, confusion set in. Belladonna thought that 4NT showed fantastic spade support and asked partner to cue bid.

(4) But Garozzo thought that 4NT was Blackwood.

After this windfall, the World Championship went to North America by the narrow margin of 413–408 imp. You can imagine how the Italian pair must have felt when they realised that they had thrown away the world title. I felt deep sympathy for them in their misfortune, but I could not help thinking that the basic trouble lay in the complicated bidding methods which the Italians employed: after the strain of a long and gruelling Championship, the last thing you need is a potential bidding misunderstanding on the 175th board of a 176-board final.

ATTRACTIVE MODERN DEVELOPMENTS

The fact that I have always remained faithful to my natural Acol-style bidding methods and have not been tempted to jump on to the Strong Club bandwagon does not mean that I do not keep a watchful eye on all the modern developments. The vast majority of the many new gadgets which descend upon the unsuspecting world each year disappear almost as quickly as they arrive, sometimes because they are too complicated for everyday use and sometimes because they have such a low frequency in practical play that it is not worth learning them. From time to time, however, new methods are introduced which constitute a genuine step forward and which really do improve the accuracy of the bidding of a substantial number of hands.

In my view, there have been two important developments of this kind in recent years. I am certain that both of them are here to stay, and I have had no hesitation in grafting them on to the simple bidding system which I like to play with my many partners. These are Jacoby Transfer Bids over 1NT and 2NT, and Herbert Negatives to Acol Two opening bids.

Jacoby Transfer Bids

The basic idea behind Jacoby Transfer Bids is an extremely simple one. Apart from two clubs, which is normally retained as Stayman, all two-level suit responses to an opening bid of 1NT are transfer bids, requesting the opener to convert to the next higher-ranking suit. Thus a response of two diamonds asks the opener to bid two hearts, and a response of two hearts requests a conversion to two spades. A response of two spades, which now becomes superfluous in a natural sense, can be given a number of possible meanings, depending on your personal taste. It can, for example, be a Baron enquiry, asking the opener to bid four-card suits in ascending order; it can be a transfer to three clubs; alternatively, it can be the prelude to a try for game in a minor suit. It can, in fact, mean anything you want it to mean, and the only important point is that you should make good use of what would otherwise be an idle response.

   The two enormous advantages to be derived from incorporating the transfer principle into the initial responses to 1NT are as follows:

   (*a*) It means that the opening bidder will probably become the declarer no matter whether the final contract is played in no trumps or in a suit. The opening lead will therefore be coming into, rather than through, the opening bidder's honours and tenaces, and this will often be worth a trick and/or a tempo to the declaring side. This factor is particularly important if you follow my advice and play a strong no trump, at least when you are vulnerable. It is to be expected that a hand containing 16–18 high-card points will contain a number of tenace holdings and unsupported honours, and transfer responses are therefore particularly valuable opposite a strong 1NT opening bid.

   (*b*) It enables the responder to describe his hand with a far greater degree of accuracy opposite a 1NT opening. For example, suppose that your partner opens 1NT, showing 16–18 points, and that you hold the following hand:

$$\spadesuit\ 2$$
$$\heartsuit\ \text{A 10 9 4 3}$$
$$\diamondsuit\ \text{K Q 7 2}$$
$$\clubsuit\ \text{J 9 3}$$

Playing traditional methods, there are not many avenues open to you. You have to jump to three hearts in order to create a forcing situation: if your partner raises to four hearts, you can be fairly hopeful that this will be the correct game contract. If he bids 3NT over three hearts, on the other hand, you will have an awkward guess to make: to push on to four diamonds might take your side out of the only makeable game contract, while to pass 3NT might work out very badly if your partner's spade holding leaves a little to be desired.

   Your task will become much easier if you are playing transfer responses to 1NT. You bid two diamonds, showing a five-card or longer heart suit and asking your partner to convert to two hearts. You then proceed with three diamonds, which is natural and forcing, and you will find that you have been able to show both your suits without taking the bidding beyond the three-level. If the opener bids 3NT in the sequence 1NT–2$\diamondsuit$–2$\heartsuit$–3$\diamondsuit$–3NT, you can be almost certain that that will be the best contract.

Similarly:

♠ 8 3
♡ K 10 8 7 4
♢ A 10 2
♣ 10 9 4

If you hold the above hand opposite a strong 1NT, you have an awkward decision to take under normal methods. A response of two hearts would be a so-called 'weakness take-out', and would end the auction; a jump to three hearts would be forcing to game, and therefore an overstatement of such modest values; a Stayman two clubs enquiry would succeed in locating a 5–4 heart fit but would otherwise be unproductive; and a raise to 2NT, while at least being a game invitation, would conceal the five-card heart suit.

The solution to this problem once again lies in Jacoby Transfers. To bid two diamonds and then convert your partner's obligatory two hearts to 2NT shows this hand exactly: a balanced hand containing a five-card heart suit and 7 or 8 points. After this illuminating bidding, the opener should be in a good position to judge whether to play in 2NT, 3NT, three hearts or four hearts.

Here is an example of transfer bids in action. This hand occurred during a semi-final match in the 1978 Helena Rubinstein Women's Teams Championship in Eastbourne, and it also shows how important it is to count accurately when you are playing bridge at any level.

Dealer South; game all.

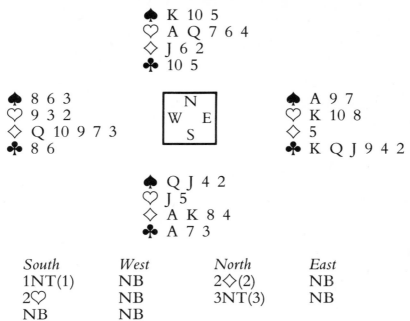

	South	West	North	East
	South	*West*	*North*	*East*
	1NT(1)	NB	2◇(2)	NB
	2♡	NB	3NT(3)	NB
	NB	NB		

(1) Showing 15–17 points.

(2) A transfer bid, requesting the opener to convert to two hearts.

(3) Showing five hearts and a balanced hand, almost certainly 5–3–3–2.

West led the 10 of diamonds against 3NT, and dummy's jack held the first trick. The correct play would seem to be to knock out the ace of spades and subsequently rely on the heart finesse but, possibly aided by some revealing hesitations during the bidding, declarer tried the effect of a low heart from dummy at the second trick. East could clearly have defeated the contract by going in with the king of hearts and switching to a club, but this would be incorrect in certain situations. East therefore ducked the first heart, and declarer's jack held the trick.

If she had recounted her tricks at this point, South would have found that she had 9 by knocking out the ace of spades: three spades, two hearts, three diamonds and one club. However, she took her eye off the ball and carelessly played a heart to the queen, giving East a second opportunity to find the killing club switch. This time she did not fail, and South ended up 3 down. I am against opening 1NT on South's hand; it does not qualify for a strong NT.

Transfer responses can also work extremely well after a 2NT opening, for they ensure that the strong hand remains concealed and that the opening lead comes into, rather than through, the honours and tenaces held by the opening bidder. Here is a typical example of what I mean. The following hand occurred during a dinner and bridge party which I attended at the house of the Moroccan Prime Minister when I visited his country for the Tangiers International Bridge Festival in 1975.

Dealer South; game all.

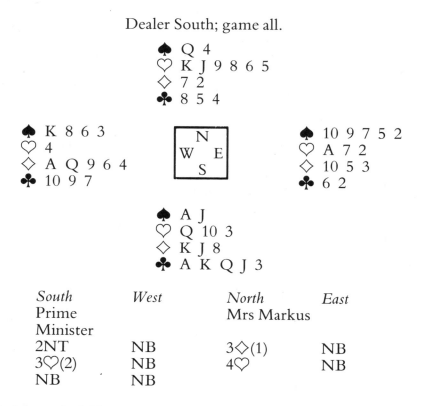

	♠ Q 4	
	♡ K J 9 8 6 5	
	◇ 7 2	
	♣ 8 5 4	

♠ K 8 6 3		♠ 10 9 7 5 2
♡ 4	N	♡ A 7 2
◇ A Q 9 6 4	W E	◇ 10 5 3
♣ 10 9 7	S	♣ 6 2

	♠ A J	
	♡ Q 10 3	
	◇ K J 8	
	♣ A K Q J 3	

South	West	North	East
Prime		Mrs Markus	
Minister			
2NT	NB	3◇(1)	NB
3♡(2)	NB	4♡	NB
NB	NB		

(1) A transfer bid, requesting partner to convert to three hearts.

(2) I must confess that I was slightly anxious when I bid three diamonds, but I need not have worried. Four hearts could not be defeated played from the South hand, for the defence could not establish a spade trick in time. We actually lost one heart and two diamonds to score +620, and this was the only plus score recorded on the North–South cards. At the other tables, the contracts were 3NT by South, one down after an opening diamond lead, and four hearts by North, one down after an opening spade lead.

Herbert Responses to Acol Two Bids

In traditional Acol, the negative response to an opening bid of two diamonds, two hearts or two spades was 2NT. This was never entirely satisfactory, for two reasons. First, it meant that a final contract of 3NT would be played from the weak hand, with the strong hand exposed on the table and the opening lead coming through its high honours. And second, it often wasted a round of bidding and made it difficult for the opener to describe his hand at a reasonable level.

Salvation has come in the shape of Herbert Responses to Acol Twos. Just as two diamonds has always been the negative reply to two clubs, the suggestion is that the negative response to an Acol Two in diamonds, hearts or spades should be a bid of the next higher-ranking suit: that is, two hearts over two diamonds, two spades over two hearts and three clubs over two spades. If the responder wishes to make a positive response in the Herbert suit, he saves space by bidding 2NT. This simple device overcomes the two principal disadvantages of the 2NT negative, and it works well on hands like the following, which occurred during the Oxford University versus Cambridge University match in 1978.

Dealer North; game all.

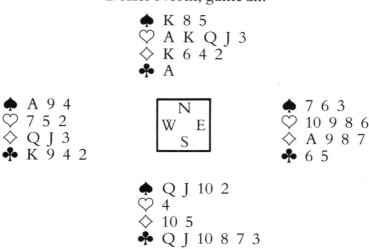

```
                    ♠ K 8 5
                    ♡ A K Q J 3
                    ♢ K 6 4 2
                    ♣ A

    ♠ A 9 4           ┌─────┐           ♠ 7 6 3
    ♡ 7 5 2           │  N  │           ♡ 10 9 8 6
    ♢ Q J 3           │W   E│           ♢ A 9 8 7
    ♣ K 9 4 2         │  S  │           ♣ 6 5
                      └─────┘
                    ♠ Q J 10 2
                    ♡ 4
                    ♢ 10 5
                    ♣ Q J 10 8 7 3
```

When Cambridge held the North–South cards, they did extremely well to chalk up a plus score in three clubs. The Oxford North–South pair came to rest in the contract which most pairs would probably reach.

South	West	North	East
		1♡	NB
1♠	NB	3◇	NB
3NT	NB	NB	NB

West led the two of clubs against 3NT, but he switched to the queen of diamonds when he gained the lead with the ace of spades and South was two down: he had to lose one spade, one club and four diamonds.

In some ways, Oxford were a little unlucky on this board, for 3NT would often make on the North–South hands. It is certainly not an attractive contract, however, particularly with the strong hand exposed on the table, and I am not keen on North's bidding. Playing Acol Twos with Herbert Negatives, I would open two hearts on the North hand, and the full sequence would be:

South	West	North	East
		2♡	NB
2♠(1)	NB	2NT(2)	NB
3NT	NB	NB	NB

(1) A Herbert Negative.

(2) Not forcing, and showing a balanced hand containing a six-card or strong five-card heart suit. Notice that a rebid of this kind would be impossible without the benefit of Herbert Negatives.

I would certainly fancy my chances of making 3NT from North's side of the table.

The Herbert system of responses to Acol Twos can also have the effect of arranging for a high-level suit contract to be played from the right side of the table. Here is an interesting illustration of this principle, taken from a Philip Morris European Cup heat in Brussels.

West	*East*
♠ K Q J 10	♠ A 9 8 7 4
♡ A K Q 10 7	♡ 8 3
◇ K 4	◇ 7 5 2
♣ K 7	♣ A 10 9

West	*East*
2♡	2NT(1)
4NT(2)	5♡
6♠	NB

(1) A positive response, showing a spade suit. Remember that a response of two spades would have been negative.
(2) Blackwood.

Notice that six spades is very likely to make when it is played from the West hand, whereas six spades by East might be scuppered by an opening diamond lead through the king.

The other significant advantage to be gained from playing Herbert Negatives occurs after an opening bid of two diamonds. If you are lucky enough to pick up a hand like this:

West
♠ A K J 4
♡ 7 2
◇ A K Q 10 8 3
♣ 4

the bidding might well proceed:

West	*East*
2◇	2♡(1)
2♠	

(1) A Herbert Negative response.

A smooth economical sequence of this kind would not be possible if East were compelled to bid 2NT as a negative response.

NOT SO ATTRACTIVE MODERN DEVELOPMENTS

Generally speaking, only the best of the new ideas in the field of bidding, like Jacoby Transfers and Herbert Negatives to Acol Twos, survive the test of time. Most of the inferior modern developments remain popular only for a short while before vanishing into obscurity, but there are, I regret, one or two exceptions to this general rule. Two of my least favourite conventions, which nevertheless seem destined to be with us for a considerable time, are the Sputnik or Negative Double and the Multi Two Diamonds opening bid.

The Sputnik Double

The basic principle of the Sputnik Double is that an immediate double of an intervening overcall is no longer for penalties, but is a take-out device, suggesting length in the two unbid suits. The level at which Sputnik Doubles operate is a matter for individual partnership agreement. In its simplest form, Sputnik only applies after an opening bid of one club or one diamond and an overcall of one spade, when a double by the responder suggests a heart suit which he cannot introduce at the two-level. However, the principle can be expanded to: (a) all overcalls which cut out a major-suit response (e.g. 1♡–2♣ but not 1♠–2◇); (b) all overcalls up to and including two spades; or (c) all overcalls at any level.

There are clearly some hands on which a Sputnik Double makes life easier for the opener's partner. For example:

North
♠ 7 2
♡ A 10 9 3
◇ K J 7 4
♣ 4 3 2

South	*West*	*North*	*East*
1♣	1♠	?	

Under normal methods, North will have to be content with a raise to two clubs on rather inadequate trump support. A Sputnik Double, inviting his partner to introduce one of the red suits as an alternative to rebidding his own suit or rebidding 1NT, obviously describes the North hand admirably. That is an entry on the plus side for Sputnik Doubles. Unfortunately, there are two major drawbacks to the system and, in my view, the disadvantages outweigh the possible advantages by quite a large margin. The snags are as follows:

(*a*) To play Sputnik Doubles inevitably means that you will lose some lucrative penalty doubles of low level contracts. Such doubles can be extremely important in match-pointed pairs contests, and they can also be a good money-spinner at the rubber bridge table. I am pleased to be able to report that the following deal occurred when I was playing for money.

Dealer North; love all.

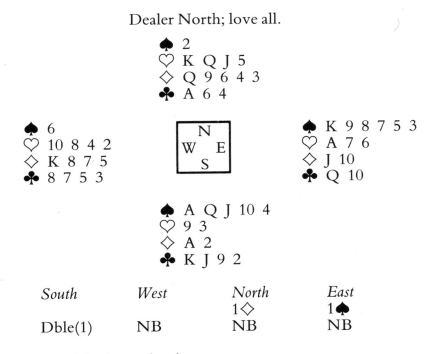

	South	West	North	East
			1◇	1♠
	Dble(1)	NB	NB	NB

(1) For penalties in my book.

I led the 2 of clubs to my partner's ace, won the club return with the king and switched to my small diamond. Not surprisingly, East misguessed, and North won with the queen and returned another club, ruffed by declarer. A small spade lost to my ten, and I cashed the ace of diamonds before playing the queen of spades, driving out East's king. Declarer now tried the effect of ducking a heart, and North won with the jack and returned a third diamond, on which East and I both discarded hearts. East now tried to cross to the ace of hearts, but I ruffed and cashed two top trumps to make the defensive tally nine tricks. That was +500 together with +100 for honours, and we were more than recompensed for the non-vulnerable game which we did not bid.

The last hand could be dubbed My Answer to the Sputnik Double. Here is another, this time from the 1984 International Bridge Festival in Juan-les-Pins.

Dealer West; North–South vulnerable.

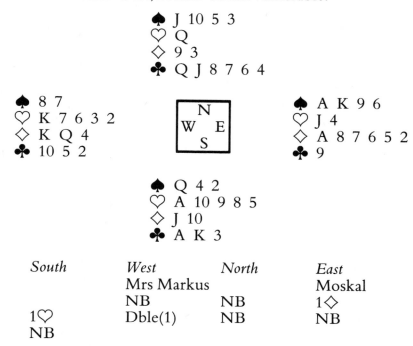

♠ J 10 5 3
♥ Q
♦ 9 3
♣ Q J 8 7 6 4

♠ 8 7   ♠ A K 9 6
♥ K 7 6 3 2   ♥ J 4
♦ K Q 4   ♦ A 8 7 6 5 2
♣ 10 5 2   ♣ 9

♠ Q 4 2
♥ A 10 9 8 5
♦ J 10
♣ A K 3

South	West	North	East
	Mrs Markus		Moskal
	NB	NB	1♦
1♥	Dble(1)	NB	NB
NB			

(1) As you will see, my partners and I play penalty doubles after our side has opened the bidding. I have to confess, however, that I was not completely certain that I was doing the right thing on this occasion, for my intermediate trumps were indifferent and too many of my values lay in partner's suit.

I led my two top diamonds against one heart doubled, and Joe Moskal overtook the second round with the ace and switched to his singleton club. Declarer won in the closed hand and led a small heart to dummy's queen, which held the trick. She then played a spade from dummy, and East went up with the king, cashed the ace of spades and gave me a third-round ruff. I returned the 10 of clubs, a McKenney suit-preference signal calling for a further spade lead, and my partner ruffed and returned his last spade. South ruffed with the 9 of hearts, and I did not make the mistake of over-ruffing: by discarding my last club at this point, I was able to ensure an additional trump trick and a penalty of +500 – a penalty which would not have been forthcoming if we had been playing Sputnik Doubles.

(*b*) To play Sputnik Doubles permits your opponents to muddy your bidding waters by making featherweight overcalls. I know this to be true for, as you will see from the following hand from the Teams Championship at the 1983 International Bridge Festival in Deauville, I do it myself.

Dealer East; love all.

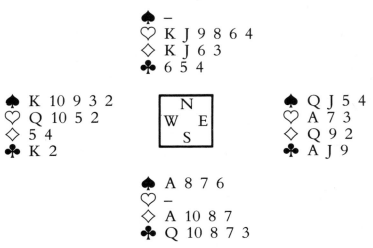

```
                    ♠ —
                    ♡ K J 9 8 6 4
                    ◇ K J 6 3
                    ♣ 6 5 4

  ♠ K 10 9 3 2        ┌─────────┐        ♠ Q J 5 4
  ♡ Q 10 5 2          │    N    │        ♡ A 7 3
  ◇ 5 4               │ W     E │        ◇ Q 9 2
  ♣ K 2               │    S    │        ♣ A J 9
                      └─────────┘
                    ♠ A 8 7 6
                    ♡ —
                    ◇ A 10 8 7
                    ♣ Q 10 8 7 3
```

At my table, the bidding was as follows:

South Mrs Markus	West	North Balian	East
			1♣(1)
1♠(2)	Dble(3)	NB	1NT
2♣	NB	NB	NB

(1) East–West were playing five-card majors, as do so many French pairs.

(2) My overcall was completely unsound, but I thought it might have a disruptive effect and I knew that my opponents' bidding methods would make it difficult for them to double me.

(3) A Sputnik Double, showing certain values and support for the unbid major suit, hearts.

I managed to make ten tricks in clubs, scoring +130. At the other table, our team-mates were armed with good, old-fashioned penalty doubles.

South	West	North	East
	Plessner		Hackett
			1♢(1)
1♠	Dble	2♡	Dble
3♣	Dble	NB	NB
3♢(2)	Dble	NB	NB
4♣	Dble(3)	NB	NB
NB			

(1) Hackett and Plessner were also playing five-card majors.
(2) North–South were for a short while in their best denomination.
(3) The fifth and final penalty double.

Henri Plessner found the excellent lead of the king of clubs against four clubs doubled. This enabled the defence to play three rounds of trumps, and declarer ended up losing two clubs and three spades.

The Multi-Coloured Two Diamonds Opening

The basic idea of the Multi-Coloured, or 'Multi', Two Diamonds is that an opening bid of two diamonds can show a number of different types of hand. Individual partnerships have different ideas on the subject, but a typical structure is that two diamonds can be based on: (a) a weak two bid in either major suit; (b) a strong two bid in either minor suit; or (c) a strong balanced hand, containing 23–24 points.

The Multi Two Diamonds has proved to be a remarkably popular convention. What is more, it has proved to be surprisingly successful, but I am absolutely certain that this is largely because too many pairs do not bother to agree a defence to the Multi and therefore find themselves nonplussed when they come across one at the table.

As well as being an undesirable addition to the game, in that any two-way bid which can be either very strong or very weak tends to give its exponents an unfair edge over average or below-average opposition, the Multi Two Diamonds seems to me to be fundamentally unsound as a pre-emptive weapon, for the following reasons:

(*a*) To open two diamonds on a weak two hand, rather than the normal two hearts or two spades, deprives the opponents of less bidding space and is therefore a less effective pre-empt.

(*b*) To open two diamonds rather than two hearts or two spades gives the next player two bites at the cherry, so to speak: he can choose between taking immediate action over two diamonds and waiting until the two diamond bidder has revealed the exact nature of his hand. I shall return to this important point when I talk about defending against the Multi Two Diamonds in the next chapter.

(*c*) One situation in which a weak two opening bid can be extremely effective arises when the responder is able to make a pre-emptive raise to the three- or four-level. For example:

South	*West*	*North*	*East*
2♠	NB	4♠	?

Unless East has a hugely powerful hand, he will often be unable to tell whether North has bid four spades to make or merely to heighten the pre-emptive effect of the weak two opening. After a Multi Two Diamond opening, it will be much more difficult for the responder to pre-empt or compete so effectively, for he will never know for certain what kind of hand his partner holds.

The following deal from the Pairs Championship at the 1982 Cannes Bridge Festival illustrates the sort of problems which the responder has to face opposite an ill-defined bid like the Multi.

Dealer East; North–South vulnerable.

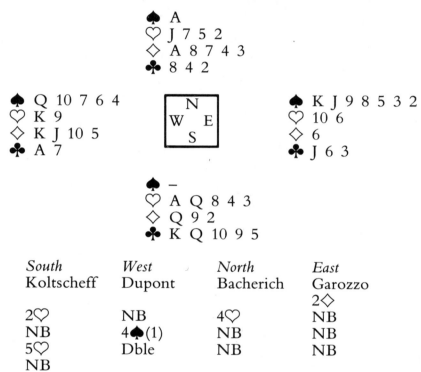

South	West	North	East
Koltscheff	Dupont	Bacherich	Garozzo
			2◇
2♡	NB	4♡	NB
NB	4♠(1)	NB	NB
5♡	Dble	NB	NB
NB			

(1) By this time, West was fairly certain that her partner's two diamond bid was based on a weak two in spades. Notice that West had been unable to take any sensible part in the auction on the previous round; I personally would hate to play any convention which meant that I had to rely on my opponents to tell me what my partner's bidding meant.

West led a spade against five hearts doubled, and the Danish star Alex Koltscheff won with the ace, discarding a diamond from the closed hand. He immediately played a club to the king and ace and West, who was already partially end-played, found the best return of a club to the jack and queen. South now found the key play of the ace and another heart, and West was end-played for a second time, and on this occasion fatally: she was forced to concede a ruff and discard in spades or to return a diamond from her king, and in either case South's diamond loser would disappear.

Finally, here is one more illustration of the problems which can arise when the responder is uncertain about the exact nature of his partner's two diamond opening. This is a not-too-serious example, but I did not feel the same way about it at the time.

Dealer West; North–South vulnerable.

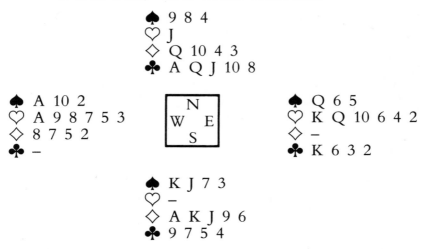

♠ 9 8 4
♡ J
◇ Q 10 4 3
♣ A Q J 10 8

♠ A 10 2
♡ A 9 8 7 5 3
◇ 8 7 5 2
♣ —

♠ Q 6 5
♡ K Q 10 6 4 2
◇ —
♣ K 6 3 2

♠ K J 7 3
♡ —
◇ A K J 9 6
♣ 9 7 5 4

When this deal occurred in an important teams event, my partner and I did a little too much at our table:

South	West	North	East
	NB	1♣	1♡
2♢	4♡	5♢	5♡
6♢	NB	NB	NB

This cost us −300, but I was not unduly worried when I realised that East–West could have scored +480 in five hearts or even +980 in six. Our team-mates at the other table, who shall remain nameless, had recently taken up the Multi Two Diamonds convention. They succeeded in keeping North–South out of the auction, but . . .

South	West	North	East
	2♢(1)	NB	2♠(2)
NB	3♣(3)	NB	3♠(4)
NB	4♠(5)	NB	NB(6)
NB			

(1) A Multi Two Diamonds, based on this occasion on a weak two in hearts.
(2) 'If you have a weak two in spades, two spades will be high enough; if you have any other kind of hand, I wish to play in a higher contract.'
(3) 'I have a minimum weak two in hearts.'
(4) 'Are you sure you don't mean spades, partner?'
(5) 'I'm happy to play in game if you have a reasonable spade suit.'
(6) 'Just as I thought. You meant to rebid three diamonds, not three clubs, showing a minimum weak two in spades.'

Four spades went three down. And nothing I have seen since has restored my faith in the convention.

2 Countering Artificiality

When I was in Seattle in the autumn of 1984 to work on the Bulletin of the Seventh World Bridge Olympiad, I was dismayed to find that there was a complete free-for-all so far as bidding systems and gadgets were concerned. For example, there were a number of pairs whose basic bidding methods were purely destructive in that, in an attempt to confuse the opposition, they passed in first and second position on all good hands and opened on all bad hands. There were also pre-emptive opening bids which had several possible meanings, opening two bids which could be weak or strong, and so on. All in all, therefore, I was not altogether sorry that I was present at the Olympiad in a journalistic capacity and did not need to fight my way through all the mumbo-jumbo at the table.

Fortunately, the most outlandish of these freak systems and conventions have not yet been licensed for general use in tournaments in England, and, as things now stand, you are only really likely to encounter them in newspaper and magazine articles. However, there are a number of blatantly artificial devices which are in fairly common use in Britain. In particular, there are two against which you really must plan your counter-measures if you are not to be at a serious disadvantage when you come across them in actual play – the strong one club opening bid, which is the keystone of the Blue Club and Precision Club systems, and the Multi-Coloured Two Diamonds opening bid. It is to be hoped that the following notes will help you sort out your defensive measures with your regular partners.

DEFENCE TO STRONG ONE CLUB BIDS

Before we consider the best action to take after one of the opponents has opened with a strength-showing one club bid, I would like to mention my general philosophy of bidding against artificial one club systems. Playing against partnerships employing the Blue or Precision Club, I have found by experience that it pays to get in first, and I always make a point of opening the bidding light first, second or third in hand provided that I have a good, rebiddable suit. I have never really analysed the reason why this approach works so well. It may be, I suppose, that a lot of players who use artificial one club systems rely on the automatic parrot-like sequences which follow and become slightly nonplussed if they are no longer able to lean on their 'crutches' when they have good hands. Whatever the reason, I can only repeat that my policy of light opening bids works remarkably well in practice.

Here is an example which occurred when I was playing with the Austrian expert, Karl Rohan, in a Pairs Tournament in Salzburg.

South dealt at love all.

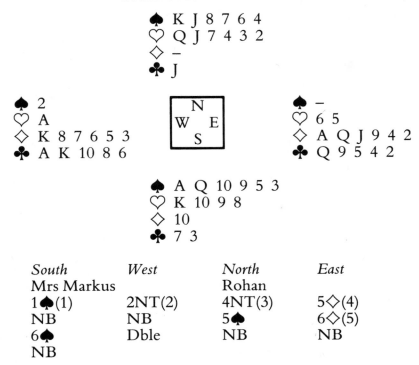

South	West	North	East
Mrs Markus		Rohan	
1♠(1)	2NT(2)	4NT(3)	5◇(4)
NB	NB	5♠	6◇(5)
6♠	Dble	NB	NB
NB			

(1) East–West had announced that they were playing a strong club system, and I adopted my normal counter-measure.

(2) The so-called Unusual Two No Trumps, showing both minor suits.

(3) North suspected that our side had few defensive values, and this was a clever attempt to bluff East–West out of a high-level minor suit contract.

(4) East was more than a little surprised by the turn of events; he should probably have taken stronger action at this point.

(5) Pleased to have an opportunity to catch up.

We would, of course, have sacrificed in seven spades if the opponents had pushed on to seven diamonds. Minus 300, or −500 if West finds the brilliant defence of cashing the ace of hearts and switching to a small club, would have been a good save; −100 in six spades doubled was even better.

Let me make it quite clear at this point that I am not biased against any system which is effective, no matter whether it is basically natural or basically artificial. Moreover, I am fully aware that a number of the world's top partnerships have done extremely well playing either the Blue Club or Precision Club system.

My contention is that these partnerships would probably have done just as well playing any other logically-constructed system. In fact, I could list a number of occasions on which I have converted strong club players to natural methods in order to play in specific tournaments and events with me, and on which we have performed extremely well with very few bidding misunderstandings or muddles.

Furthermore, I contend that natural bidding systems tend to work very much better than artificial systems in competitive auctions. I am quite prepared to believe, for example, that the Precision Club system works extremely well if you are simply bidding hands in the comfort of your armchair at home, without the inconvenience of having two opponents to make nuisances of themselves. At the actual table, however, it has always seemed to me that, since the strong clubbers have to devote the first round of bidding to showing their points and/or controls, they are inevitably very vulnerable to pre-emption by well-organised and determined opponents. To be able to start the auction with a strength-showing bid of one club works well on certain hands; it does not work so well, however, if vigorous interference bidding compels the opening side to make intelligent guesses at the correct final contract before they have any indication of the distribution of their two hands or of the whereabouts of their high cards.

It follows from this that my basic policy over an artificial one club opening is to bid as much and as often as possible whenever I have a weak or indifferent hand. Over one club, I like to employ the following structure of overcalls:

(*a*) A double or triple jump overcall, for example 1♣–3◇ or 1♣–4♡, is pre-emptive, showing a long suit and five or six other cards. These bids are extremely difficult to counter when the opening side has made absolutely no progress towards describing the nature or distribution of their hands; moreover, this same lack of knowledge can be critical in the defence if they elect to double the pre-emptive overcall. Here is a case in point from the 1983 Juan-les-Pins International Bridge Festival, in which I played with Austria's Maria Kirner, one of the top woman players in Europe.

Dealer North; East–West vulnerable.

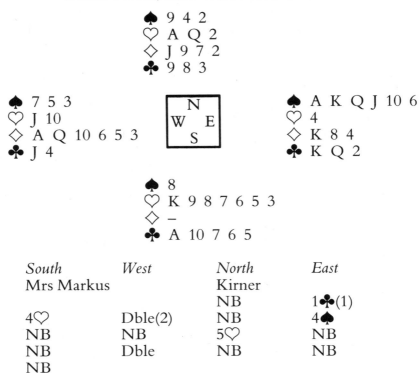

| ♠ 9 4 2 |
| ♡ A Q 2 |
| ◇ J 9 7 2 |
| ♣ 9 8 3 |

South	West	North	East
Mrs Markus		Kirner	
		NB	1♣(1)
4♡	Dble(2)	NB	4♠
NB	NB	5♡	NB
NB	Dble	NB	NB
NB			

(1) East–West were playing the Precision Club system, and one club therefore showed any hand containing 16 or more points.

(2) Showing some values.

West led a spade against five hearts doubled, and I ruffed the second round and played five rounds of trumps, discarding two clubs from dummy. Not having the slightest idea where his partner's high cards or long suit lay, the unfortunate East eventually abandoned the two of clubs. This enabled me to play the ace and another club to establish the long clubs and make my doubled contract. Since East–West were likely to make +650 in spades, I could actually afford to go three down in five hearts doubled and still show a profit. As it was, +650 on the North–South cards gave us a top score on the board.

(*b*) A jump overcall, for example 1♣–2♡, shows a good suit but less than opening values; in other words, it shows the sort of hand which would be full value for a weak two opening. For example:

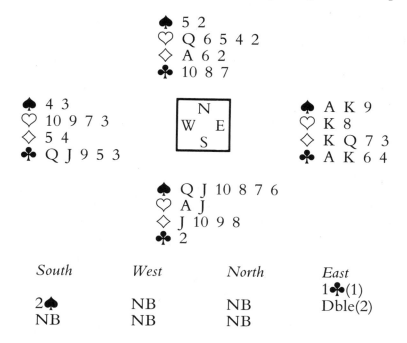

```
                    ♠ 5 2
                    ♡ Q 6 5 4 2
                    ◇ A 6 2
                    ♣ 10 8 7

   ♠ 4 3                              ♠ A K 9
   ♡ 10 9 7 3          N             ♡ K 8
   ◇ 5 4            W     E          ◇ K Q 7 3
   ♣ Q J 9 5 3         S             ♣ A K 6 4

                    ♠ Q J 10 8 7 6
                    ♡ A J
                    ◇ J 10 9 8
                    ♣ 2
```

South	West	North	East
			1♣(1)
2♠	NB	NB	Dble(2)
NB	NB	NB	

(1) A Precision Club opening, as before.

(2) It was tempting for East to double, but he should have realised that the defenders are bound to be severely handicapped when all their points are concentrated in one hand. High-card strength is always more effective when it is fairly evenly divided between the two partners.

Two spades doubled could never be defeated on this deal. Careful defence would have held me to eight tricks, but East allowed himself to be end-played and I emerged with an overtrick and a score of +570.

(*c*) A simple overcall, for example 1♣–1♠, is purely and simply a nuisance bid, designed to disrupt the flow of the opponents' auction; it therefore shows no particular values, especially not vulnerable.

My policy on good hands over a conventional one club opening bid is to pass on the first round. The key point on such hands is to listen to the bidding and discover from the initial response to one club and from the opener's rebid which side is likely to hold the balance of the high cards and who is likely to hold the missing points which are not in my hand and are not part of the opener's basic 16. If it becomes clear that the deal does not belong to the opening side, my plan is to enter the auction on the second round; if, on the other hand, it transpires that my partner is almost certain to be a broken reed, I am happy to stay out of the bidding and not give the eventual declarer any indication of the lie of the adverse cards.

To bid immediately over one club on good hands makes it impossible for the defending side to judge how far to go in the auction. It is much easier for the overcaller's partner to plan his disruptive action if he is certain that he is opposite a hand of limited strength. The Pakistani champion, Zia Mahmoud, waged an effective campaign on the following deal from the final of the 1984 Philip Morris European Cup in Monte Carlo.

Dealer South; game all.

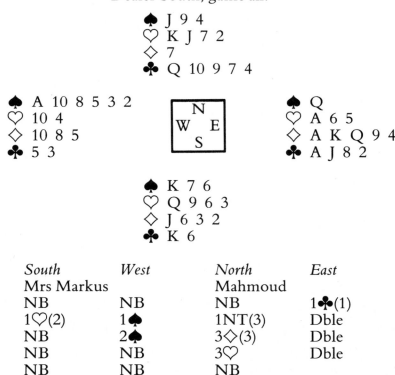

♠ J 9 4
♡ K J 7 2
♢ 7
♣ Q 10 9 7 4

♠ A 10 8 5 3 2   ♠ Q
♡ 10 4   ♡ A 6 5
♢ 10 8 5   ♢ A K Q 9 4
♣ 5 3   ♣ A J 8 2

♠ K 7 6
♡ Q 9 6 3
♢ J 6 3 2
♣ K 6

South	West	North	East
Mrs Markus		Mahmoud	
NB	NB	NB	1♣(1)
1♡(2)	1♠	1NT(3)	Dble
NB	2♠	3♢(3)	Dble
NB	NB	3♡	Dble
NB	NB	NB	

(1) A Precision Club bid, showing 16 or more points and any distribution.

(2) My hand was really far too balanced for a vulnerable overcall, but I cannot always resist this kind of temptation.

(3) Zia's antics were all designed to confuse the opponents; he thought it would be safe to retreat to three hearts if I had anything approaching a reasonable overcall.

West led a club against three hearts doubled, and East went up with the ace and returned a club to my king. Trying hard to appear unconcerned, I played a heart to dummy's jack and East's ace. East now switched to the queen of spades, and West captured my king with the ace and, still seeking a club ruff, switched to a diamond. East won with the queen and returned a club, and I suddenly realised that I was in with a chance.

I ruffed the third club with the queen of hearts and played a trump to dummy's king, felling West's doubleton 10. A trump to the 9, which drew East's last trump, was followed by a spade to dummy's 9, and I was home: dummy was left with the jack of spades, two winning clubs and the 13th trump, and that was +730 to our side.

I should perhaps mention at this point that, while I do not use such methods myself, I can see quite a compelling case for playing some kind of two-suited overcalling system over strong one club bids. If the overcaller is able to show two four-card or longer suits by his first bid, he effectively doubles the chances of his partner being able to make a pre-emptive raise in response. One such structure of intervening bids is known as the Truscott Defence, the basic principle of which is that all simple overcalls show the suit named plus the next higher-ranking suit, with double and 1NT covering the non-touching suit combinations. Thus:

OVER ONE CLUB
1♢ shows diamonds and hearts
1♡ shows hearts and spades
1♠ shows spades and clubs
1NT shows diamonds and spades
2♣ shows clubs and diamonds
Double shows clubs and hearts

OVER ONE CLUB–ONE DIAMOND (NEGATIVE)
1♡ shows hearts and spades
1♠ shows spades and clubs
1NT shows clubs and hearts
2♣ shows clubs and diamonds
2♢ shows diamonds and hearts
Double shows diamonds and spades

The disadvantages of such methods are, of course, that (a) you are forced to either pass or make a jump overcall if you have a one-suited hand, and (b) you disclose rather too much information about your distribution if the opening side eventually plays the hand. You must simply decide for yourself whether or not these disadvantages are outweighed by the additional disruption which can be caused on the basis of the two-suited overcall.

There is no doubt about the way in which the Cambridge University team decided when they were planning their tactics for the 1983 'Varsity Match. Here is an exaggerated example of a two-suited overcall in action at the table:

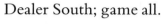

Dealer South; game all.

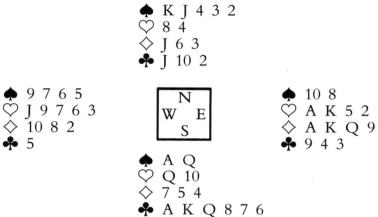

```
              ♠ K J 4 3 2
              ♡ 8 4
              ◇ J 6 3
              ♣ J 10 2
♠ 9 7 6 5        ┌───────┐       ♠ 10 8
♡ J 9 7 6 3      │   N   │       ♡ A K 5 2
◇ 10 8 2         │ W   E │       ◇ A K Q 9
♣ 5              │   S   │       ♣ 9 4 3
                 └───────┘
              ♠ A Q
              ♡ Q 10
              ◇ 7 5 4
              ♣ A K Q 8 7 6
```

When Cambridge held the North–South cards, they managed to buy the contract in three clubs, losing the obvious five tricks. Plus 100 to Oxford.

At the other table:

South	West	North	East
1♣(1)	1♡(2)	Dble(3)	3♡(4)
NB	NB	3♠	Dble
NB	NB(5)	NB	

(1) A Precision Club bid, as before.

(2) Showing hearts and spades. The younger generation clearly shares my view that it pays to enter the auction over a strong one club opening bid.

(3) Showing 5–8 points.

(4) East's three hearts was a well-judged bid. He knew that, systemically, North–South would have to bid again, either doubling three hearts or introducing a suit of their own which East would be able to double.

(5) Showing touching faith.

Three spades doubled went two down when East cashed his five red-suit winners and switched to a club, which meant that declarer could not get to his hand to draw trumps without conceding a club ruff to West. As you will see, North–South were doomed to lose at least 500 once East had bid three hearts. Four clubs doubled would also go two down, and West would make ten tricks in three hearts doubled unless North–South found the good defence of cashing the ace of clubs and playing three rounds of spades, promoting a trump trick for South.

I am sure that some of you will be contemplating the extreme examples which I have quoted here and wondering why it is that such risky interference bids appear to work so well after one club openings. It seems to me that there are three principal reasons for their success. First, the opening side normally have to decide whether or not to double the intervening bid *before* they have begun to show their long suits and to describe the general nature of their hands; this inevitably makes it difficult for them to take a sensible decision. Second, a number of doubles, particularly by the opener's partner, are needed by the strong clubbers in a Sputnik or negative sense, showing certain values rather than suggesting that the opening side should try to extract a penalty; this means that even the most hair-raising overcalls often escape unpunished. And finally, not all Precision Club and Blue Club pairs are sufficiently well organised to be able to cope with intervention effectively. While they are normally reasonably competent at reaching a sensible contract by way of their one club opening and a series of responses and rebids, most of which are automatic and require no great thought, it seems to me that the strong clubbers are all too easily thrown by active opponents.

This last point holds true at the very highest level, as is shown by the following deal from the 1981 competition for the Venice Cup, the World Ladies' Team Championship.

Dealer East; North–South vulnerable.

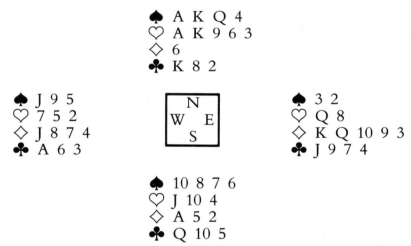

This deal occurred in the key match between USA and Great Britain. When Sally Sowter (now Sally Horton) and Sandra Landy held the North–South cards for Britain, North opened one heart, South responded one spade and they had no difficulty in reaching the correct contract of four spades.

No such natural sequence was available to the US pair at the other table, where North's Precision Club opening encountered the usual stiff resistance.

South	West Davies	North	East Gardener NB
NB	NB	1♣(1)	2◇(2)
Dble(3)	NB	2♡(4)	NB
NB(5)	NB		

(1) 16 or more points, any distribution.

(2) Nicola Gardener (now Nicola Smith) and Pat Davies were playing the so-called 'Panama' defence to the artificial one club; two diamonds showed either (a) a weak jump overcall in diamonds or (b) a 5–4–4–0 or 4–4–4–1 distribution with short diamonds.

(3) According to their system, South's double of two diamonds should have shown a balanced hand with 8 or more points and no diamond guard.

(4) In view of South's positive response, North assumed that two hearts would be forcing.

(5) Wrong again.

One final point on the subject of bidding over an artificial one club opening bid: if you follow my advice and intervene as often as you can over one club, you will occasionally make life a little difficult for your partner when you find him with a strong hand. It is for this reason that you should reserve your immediate overcalls for weakish hands, preferring to pass and bid later on good hands so that your partner will have an approximate idea of how high to go. Even if he knows that your overcall is weak, of course, he might still find it difficult to cope if he has a strong holding, particularly as he will probably not have a cue bid in the opponents' suit available. Not everyone will be able to display the same flair and judgement as Martin Hoffman did on the following hand from a small pairs event.

Dealer West; love all.

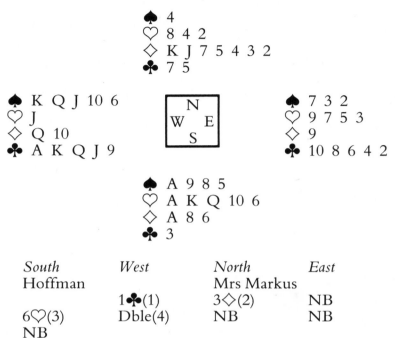

South	West	North	East
Hoffman		Mrs Markus	
	1♣(1)	3◇(2)	NB
6♡(3)	Dble(4)	NB	NB
NB			

(1) Precision.

(2) This was a little unsound but, as I have explained, I always try to make life as difficult as possible for my opponents after a conventional one club bid.

(3) Six diamonds might have been a safer bid, but Martin was conscious of the fact that this was a match-pointed pairs competition.

(4) Out of pique, no doubt.

As you will see, Martin had no difficulty in making 12 tricks after ruffing the second round of clubs: five hearts, one spade and six diamonds. Six spades or seven clubs would have been a cheap sacrifice on the East–West cards, but West was never in a position to bid either of his excellent suits in a natural sense.

DEFENCE TO THE MULTI-COLOURED TWO DIAMONDS

To my mind, one of the most inexplicable success stories in the world of tournament bridge during recent years has been that of the so-called Multi-Coloured, or 'Multi', Two Diamonds opening bid. The principle behind this bid is that an opening bid of two diamonds can be either weak or strong, and this put me off the convention right at the outset: I do not believe that the English Bridge Union should have licensed for general use any bid which might mean a weak hand containing 5–9 points but which might equally mean a strong hand containing, say, 23–24 points. The various shades of meaning vary considerably from partnership to partnership, but the types of hand shown by a Multi Two Diamonds are normally: (a) a weak two in either major suit; (b) a strong two in either minor suit; or (c) a balanced hand containing 23–24 points. Some partnerships replace category (b) or (c) with a fourth type of hand: (d) a strong three-suited hand, 4–4–4–1 or 5–4–4–0 distribution.

Advocates of the Multi Two Diamonds argue that it enables them to retain the pre-emptive effect of the weak two in either hearts or spades, while at the same time preserving immediate opening bids of two hearts and two spades as Acol Twos. I personally regard the convention as silly, dicey and unfair, but I have to admit that it has proved remarkably successful in its formative years, wreaking a certain amount of havoc amongst opponents who have not bothered to discuss their counter-measures.

In my view, the defence to the Multi Two Diamonds should be based around one of the principal disadvantages of the convention: namely, that it gives the defender immediately over the two diamond bid at least two bites at the cherry. If North–South are playing standard weak twos and South opens, say, two spades:

South	West	North	East
2♠	?		

West has to take any action which he deems necessary *now*: if he passes at his first turn, two spades may very well become the final contract.

If, on the other hand, North–South are playing the Multi and South has to open two diamonds in order to show a weak two in spades, West has two opportunities to enter the auction. He can either come in on the first round:

South	West	North	East
2◇	?		

or he can bide his time until South has clarified what type of hand he holds:

South	West	North	East
2◇	NB	2♡	NB
2♠	?		

The defending side must make the best possible use of these two opportunities to intervene over a Multi, and I would suggest a fairly simple structure of bids, along the following lines:

Bidding on the First Round

(a) *Suit Bids* Natural, suggesting a basically one-suited hand. Remember that even if you choose the wrong moment to overcall, it will not always be possible for the opener's partner to double if he does not know which major suit the two diamond bid is based on.

(b) *2NT* Natural, showing 17+ points and a guard in both major suits.

(c) *Double* An immediate double of two diamonds is probably best used to indicate that you are interested in doubling the opponents' escape suit for penalties. In fourth position, after the opener's partner has bid two of a major, a double is best used as a take-out double. Thus:

South	West	North	East
2◇	NB	2♠	Dble

East's double of two spades shows a good hand with short spades. He hopes that if South passes two spades doubled, West will have sufficient spades over South's long suit to be able to pass and convert the double into a penalty double.

This agreement on the meaning of an immediate double would have saved Oxford University a lot of points in the 1978 'Varsity Match against Cambridge, when the following spectacular disaster occurred:

```
                    ♠ 3
                    ♡ J 6 5
                    ◇ A J 10 6 3 2
                    ♣ J 6 3

  ♠ A K 10 8         ┌─────────┐         ♠ 4 2
  ♡ Q 9 7 2          │    N    │         ♡ A 10 3
  ◇ K Q 4          W │         │ E       ◇ 9 8 7 5
  ♣ A 5              │    S    │         ♣ K 8 7 2
                     └─────────┘

                    ♠ Q J 9 7 6 5
                    ♡ K 8 4
                    ◇ –
                    ♣ Q 10 9 4
```

When Oxford held the East–West cards, the bidding was a little confused, to say the least:

South	West	North	East
2◇(1)	NB(2)	2♡(3)	NB
2♠	3♣(4)	NB(5)	4♣(6)
NB	4NT(7)	NB	5◇(8)
NB	5♠(9)	NB	6♣(10)
NB	NB	NB	

(1) A Multi Two Diamonds, based on this occasion on a weak two in spades.

(2) This is the sort of hand on which I would double two diamonds, for I would be prepared to double either two hearts or two spades for penalties.

(3) Announcing that two hearts was quite high enough if partner's two diamonds were based on a weak two in hearts.

(4) West now thought that the time had come for action, but it is not clear why he did not make a penalty double of two spades. His actual bid of three clubs was meant to be for a take-out, showing the other major suit.

(5) Relieved to be off the hook.

(6) East was confused. He clearly thought that his partner's three club overcall was natural.

(7) West's 4NT bid was obviously meant to be natural, not Blackwood.

(8) However, East showed one ace.

(9) West was still trying to escape and play the hand in 5NT.

(10) However, East thought that his partner was making a grand slam try. Understandably, he declined the invitation and signed off in six.

Oxford's gallant contract of six clubs went three down, mercifully undoubled. This cautionary tale shows the kind of success which the Multi Two Diamond opening can achieve if the opponents have not done their homework and discussed how they are going to defend against it.

When you are planning your defence to the Multi Two Diamonds, or contemplating bidding over a Multi at the table, you should always assume that the opener is concealing a weak two in one of the majors: the strong meanings of two diamonds are very rare in actual play. Occasionally, of course, you will find that you have attempted to deal with a weak two when the opener actually held a strong hand, but this will not necessarily prove fatal. In fact, interference over the strong hand can work out extremely well, as on the following deal from the 1977 Guardian Easter Tournament.

Dealer West; love all.

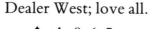

♠ A 9 6 5
♡ A 10 9 4
♢ Q J 10 5
♣ A

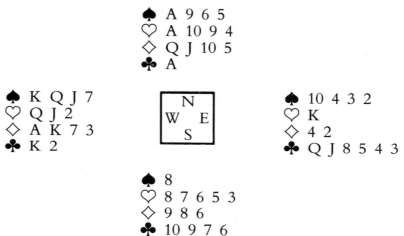

♠ K Q J 7   ♠ 10 4 3 2
♡ Q J 2   ♡ K
♢ A K 7 3   ♢ 4 2
♣ K 2   ♣ Q J 8 5 4 3

♠ 8
♡ 8 7 6 5 3
♢ 9 8 6
♣ 10 9 7 6

This was the bidding when Mrs Fritzi Gordon and the French star Leon Tintner held the North–South cards.

South Mrs Gordon	West	North Tintner	East
	2◇(1)	Dble(2)	NB
2♡(3)	Dble(4)	NB	NB
NB			

(1) A Multi Two Diamonds, based on this occasion on a strong balanced hand.

(2) Indicating a desire to defend against two hearts or two spades if West's Multi were based on a weak two in one of the major suits.

(3) Fritzi should perhaps have passed the double to await developments, but it would be churlish of me to argue with success.

(4) Showing a strong balanced hand.

South was not severely tested in the play, and +470 gave Mrs Gordon and Tintner a shared 'top' on the board.

Bidding on the Second Round

(*a*) *Suit Bids* After a first-round pass, a suit bid on the second round is still completely natural. However, it will be to some extent protective when the opponents have both advertised weak hands; for example:

South	West	North	East
2◇	NB	2♡	NB
NB	2♠		

(*b*) *2NT* After passing on the first round, it is possible to use an overcall of 2NT at your second turn as 'unusual', showing both minor suits.

(*c*) *Double* After doubling two diamonds on the first round, a double of two hearts or two spades on the second round is a penalty double.

After passing over two diamonds on the first round, a second-round double is for a take-out, showing good values.

Here is an example of a delayed take-out double. It occurred during the Guardian Easter Tournament in 1982.

Dealer North; love all.

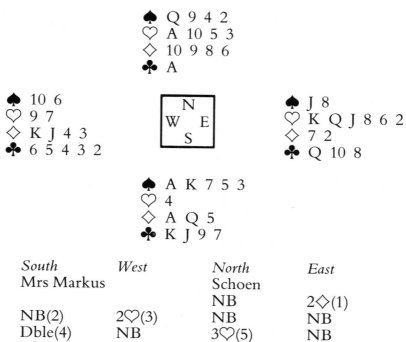

♠	Q 9 4 2		
♡	A 10 5 3		
◇	10 9 8 6		
♣	A		

♠ 10 6
♡ 9 7
◇ K J 4 3
♣ 6 5 4 3 2

♠ J 8
♡ K Q J 8 6 2
◇ 7 2
♣ Q 10 8

♠ A K 7 5 3
♡ 4
◇ A Q 5
♣ K J 9 7

South Mrs Markus	West	North Schoen	East
		NB	2◇(1)
NB(2)	2♡(3)	NB	NB
Dble(4)	NB	3♡(5)	NB
4♠	NB	NB	NB

(1) A Multi Two Diamonds, concealing on this occasion a weak two bid in hearts.

(2) I have found it is best to pass on the first round and await developments on this kind of hand. Such tactics would not be possible in fourth position, of course, for you might find that a tactical pass when you are *under* the two diamond bidder ends the auction.

(3) Showing a limited hand on which two hearts would be high enough if East's bid were based on a weak two in hearts.

(4) Showing a good hand with short hearts.

(5) North had enough for game opposite my strong bidding.

When dummy went down, I realised that six spades would make if suits broke well and the diamond honours were favourably placed. I therefore decided to assume that 12 tricks were not readily available, hoping thereby to beat all the pairs going down in slam contracts and to make more tricks than those who had lingered in game. I won the opening heart lead in dummy, drew trumps in two rounds and cashed the ace of clubs. I then ruffed a heart in the closed hand, paving the way for an elimination, and cashed the king of clubs, discarding a diamond from dummy. When the 10 of clubs appeared from East, I did not need to look any further for 12 tricks: I ran the jack of clubs, throwing another diamond from dummy, and subsequently discarded a third diamond on the established 9 of clubs. I was then able to ruff two diamonds in dummy, thereby collecting 12 tricks by way of five spades and two ruffs, one heart, one diamond and three clubs. Those declarers who ignored the club suit and settled for two diamond finesses ended up with only 11 tricks.

3   Getting into the Act

Competitive bidding is a vast subject about which I could find enough to say to fill a very large book with very little difficulty. On this occasion, however, I am only able to devote one small chapter of a medium-sized book to the whole of this complex question, and I shall therefore concentrate my attention on three specific aspects of bidding after the opponents have opened. These are the following: (a) bidding when the opponents open with a weak 1NT; (b) bidding when the opponents make a pre-emptive opening; and (c) the jump overcall.

THE OPPONENTS OPEN WITH A WEAK NO TRUMP

To put it mildly, I am not a great supporter of the weak no trump, largely because it is a gambling bid which, to my mind, is out of place in what is not basically a gambling game. To open 1NT on 12–14 points rarely helps the opening side to reach the correct part-score and, unless the responder is quite strong, it will make it absolutely impossible to reach any available 4–4 suit fit. For example:

West	*East*
♠ Q 10 7 2	♠ J 8 6 4
♡ K 5 4	♡ A Q 8 2
◇ Q 9	◇ 7 3
♣ A K 8 3	♣ 10 7 2

West has a maximum hand for 1NT, and his side has the balance of the points. However, 1NT is very unlikely to make on the East–West cards, and I would much prefer to achieve a plus score after the simple natural auction of 1♣–1♡–1♠–2♠.

The other big disadvantage of the weak 1NT is that it is so easy to double. To advertise to the world at large that you have a balanced hand containing only slightly more than your fair share of the high-card points really is asking for trouble, particularly when you are vulnerable. It therefore seems to me that those players who set themselves up as sitting ducks by opening with a weak 1NT are simply gambling that either their partner has a reasonable hand or the opponents' strength will be divided in such a way that they will find it difficult to double.

Of course, it would be unfair of me to suggest that the weak no trump has no good points. It has to be admitted that having a 1NT bid available makes it very much simpler for the opener to deal with hands like:

♠ A K 4		♠ 10 8 6 4
♡ J 7 5 2	*or*	♡ A K 5
◇ K 9 3		◇ J 7 4 2
♣ Q 7 2		♣ A J

Furthermore, an opening bid of 1NT sometimes has a useful pre-emptive effect, making it difficult for the opponents to enter the auction and find their correct part-score or, on occasions, game contract. It is because of this danger that I make it my policy not to be put off by a weak 1NT, but to get into the bidding as often as I reasonably can.

In my view, the best defence to the weak 1NT is as follows:

In Second Position

If I am sitting immediately over the opening bidder, I will always double 1NT if I can find the slightest excuse. Theoretically, a double should be based on either a fair hand with a good suit or a strong, balanced hand, but I have been known to reduce these requirements in the heat of the moment. Here, for example, is a hand from the 1984 Guardian Easter Swiss Pairs Tournament.

Dealer East; game all.

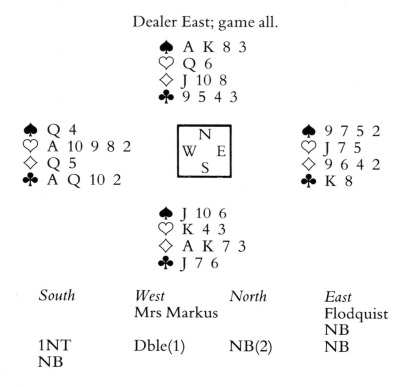

South	West	North	East
	Mrs Markus		Flodquist
			NB
1NT	Dble(1)	NB(2)	NB
NB			

(1) On reflection, mine was neither a fair hand with a good suit nor a strong, balanced hand, but I am always looking out for an opportunity to punish the weak no trump.

(2) Content, as they say in some rubber bridge circles.

I led the 10 of hearts against 1NT doubled, and I had a nasty shock when I saw dummy and when dummy's queen of hearts held the first trick. Deciding to hope for the spade finesse and break, South crossed to hand with the ace of diamonds and led the jack of spades to the queen and king. A spade to the 10 and another spade revealed the 4–2 break, and declarer now hit upon the idea of throwing me in with a club and compelling me to concede a trick in either hearts or diamonds. He therefore led a small club from dummy, but my partner was extremely alert: he went in with the king of clubs, cashed the 9 of spades and returned the jack of hearts, giving us eight defensive tricks, +500 and a very good match-point score on the board.

Generally speaking, I expect my partner to pass my double of 1NT if he has as many as 4 points. With a worse hand than that, he should probably remove the double if he has a five-card suit. With only four-card suits, however, there is a case for his standing the double even if he has 0–3 points, particularly if our side is vulnerable: to scramble around trying to escape into poor four-card suits can cost considerably more than the −180 or −380 which we would concede if 1NT doubled were made.

With insufficient values for a penalty double but a good enough hand to compete over 1NT, the second player should overcall in any reasonable six-card suit or good five-card suit. Without a biddable suit, he may need to fall back on one of the various conventional take-out devices which are so popular these days. You can take your pick from the many brands which are currently on the market – Sharples, Ripstra, Landy, Aspro, Pottage and Astro, for example. I am sure that they all have their good points, but personally I am always perfectly happy to keep all suit overcalls completely natural apart from two diamonds, which I like to use as a conventional way of showing both major suits.

One important point which I would like to emphasise in connection with these conventional take-out devices is that they should be used only if you are not strong enough to make a penalty double: if you can double 1NT, I am certain that it will pay you to do so. Failure to appreciate this point cost Oxford University a bushel of points in the 1982 'Varsity Match against Cambridge, when this deal came along:

Dealer South; game all.

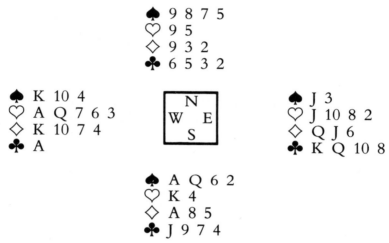

```
              ♠ 9 8 7 5
              ♡ 9 5
              ◇ 9 3 2
              ♣ 6 5 3 2

♠ K 10 4                          ♠ J 3
♡ A Q 7 6 3      N                ♡ J 10 8 2
◇ K 10 7 4    W     E             ◇ Q J 6
♣ A              S                ♣ K Q 10 8

              ♠ A Q 6 2
              ♡ K 4
              ◇ A 8 5
              ♣ J 9 7 4
```

When Oxford held the North–South cards, the bidding was as follows:

South	West	North	East
1NT(1)	Dble	2♣	Dble
NB	NB	NB	

(1) Showing 12–14 points. The weak no trump seems to have become a 'must' in the 'Varsity Match.

East led the jack of hearts against the gruesome contract of two clubs doubled, and the unfortunate declarer did remarkably well to emerge with four tricks. However, it was still +1100 to Cambridge.

At the other table, both the Oxford players chose a bad moment to underbid:

South	West	North	East
1NT	2♣(1)	NB(2)	2♡
NB	NB	NB	

(1) Astro, showing hearts and another suit. This seems to me to be a very poor alternative to the obvious penalty double.

(2) No doubt with an almost audible sigh of relief.

As you can see, the Oxford East–West pair not only missed a four-figure penalty: they also missed a vulnerable game, and they had to return to their team-mates with the ignominious score of +230.

In Fourth Position

I like to vary my defensive methods if the opening bid of 1NT is made on my left and is followed by two passes. In fourth position, I am quite happy to reduce my requirements for a penalty double to any balanced hand containing reasonable opening values. Once the third player has passed, it is quite likely that my partner has some worthwhile bits and pieces, and my double is to all intents and purposes a protective one.

I do not favour playing any conventional take-out bids in fourth position. If my hand is not strong enough to double and has no suit good enough to bid in a natural sense, my view is that I should probably be passing over 1NT in any case.

THE OPPONENTS OPEN WITH A PRE-EMPTIVE BID

Bidding Over Weak Twos

If it is reserved for use on suitable hands, the weak two can prove to be a reasonably effective pre-emptive weapon – unlike the Multi Two Diamonds which is extraordinarily popular at the present time but which I consider to be an utterly silly convention. However, I do not favour any special counter-measures over weak twos. I like to treat them in exactly the same way as I treat one bids, which means that suit overcalls are completely natural, 2NT shows a strong, balanced hand and a double is for a take-out.

Bidding Over Weak Threes

Defensive measures over weak threes come in and go out of fashion. Every generation claims to find a new and improved method of dealing with pre-emptive three bids, but the truth of the matter is that no counter-measures are really effective: that is why weak three bids have always flourished and, in my view, will continue to do so for as long as the game is played.

If anybody ever succeeds in discovering a defence to weak three bids which works, say, nine times out of ten, I should be grateful if he or she would get in touch with me immediately. In the meantime, I shall continue to employ the defensive measures which I have favoured for many years, which seem to me to work as well as any others and which have the overriding advantage of being simple:

(a) *Double* A take-out double, showing a good hand and implying support for the three unbid suits.

(b) *3NT* Natural; to play in 3NT.

(c) *All New-Suit Bids* Natural, showing a good suit.

One of the principal advantages of take-out doubles over weak three bids is that they waste no bidding space and leave as much room as possible in which the defending side can exchange information. Here is a case in point from the St Moritz Winter Tournament in January 1984, where I was playing with the great Pietro Forquet, a member of the famous Italian Blue Team which had such an incredible record in World and European Championships.

Dealer West; North–South vulnerable.

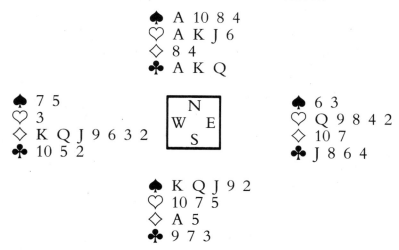

South	West	North	East
Forquet		Mrs Markus	
	3◇	Dble(1)	NB
4♠(2)	NB	5♣	NB
5◇	NB	5♡(3)	NB
6♠	NB	NB	NB

(1) A take-out double.

(2) Notice that the double leaves room for South to make a jump response without venturing beyond the game level. If North had to bid four clubs as a conventional take-out manoeuvre, for example, it would be difficult for South to show any positive values.

(3) Continuing to describe the key features of my hand and leaving the final decision to my partner.

This hand gave Pietro Forquet a chance to show why he merits the reputation of being one of the greatest living bridge players. He won the opening diamond lead with the ace, drew trumps in two rounds and cashed the three top clubs. When he discovered that West had started life with at least five black cards, declarer realised that he was most unlikely to hold more than one heart. He therefore continued by cashing the ace of hearts and exiting with a diamond. If West won the trick, he would be compelled to return a third diamond, conceding a ruff and discard; and if East won the second diamond, he would be forced to lead into dummy's heart tenace or concede a ruff and discard by returning the 13th club. In either case, declarer's heart loser was no more.

Just as important as your conventional means of entering the auction over weak threes is your general approach to the problem of how to counter them. Whether you are using take-out doubles, optional doubles, Fishbein, Herbert, Lower Minor, Three No Trumps, FILM or any other variety of conventional device, you must bear in mind the following important points when you are contemplating action over a pre-emptive three opening:

(*a*) You cannot afford to be too timid about coming in over weak threes. Unless you are resigned to allowing yourself to be talked out of game contract after game contract, you must be prepared to take a slight risk from time to time. Just as you would expect, John Collings was fully prepared to walk on thin ice on the following deal from the 1978 Cannes Bridge Festival.

Dealer East; North–South vulnerable.

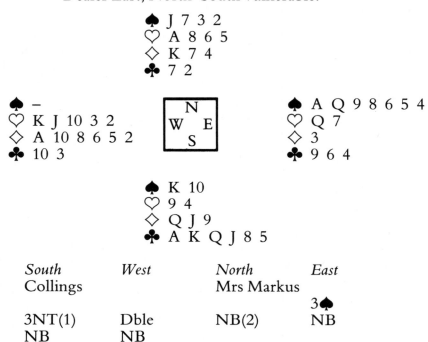

	♠ J 7 3 2	
	♡ A 8 6 5	
	◇ K 7 4	
	♣ 7 2	

♠ –		♠ A Q 9 8 6 5 4
♡ K J 10 3 2	N	♡ Q 7
◇ A 10 8 6 5 2	W E	◇ 3
♣ 10 3	S	♣ 9 6 4

	♠ K 10	
	♡ 9 4	
	◇ Q J 9	
	♣ A K Q J 8 5	

South	West	North	East
Collings		Mrs Markus	
			3♠
3NT(1)	Dble	NB(2)	NB
NB	NB		

(1) Without the slightest hesitation.

(2) I was quietly confident, but it was clear that my partner was banking on finding quite a lot in my hand.

West led a small diamond, and South won in dummy with the king and immediately led a small spade, settling for nine tricks when East won and switched to a heart.

An interesting point about this hand is that the only lead to defeat 3NT is a small heart. I have often found that it pays to lead low from holdings like K–J–10–x–x, for if partner has an honour, to lead the jack may block the defenders' suit or present declarer with a second guard therein. On this particular deal, for example, the contract can be made on the lead of the jack of hearts, for declarer can go up with the ace in dummy and drive out the ace of diamonds while the defenders' heart suit is jammed up; a small heart lead will leave East–West in full control of the situation.

(*b*) The fact that you often have to take a slight risk in order to clamber into the auction over a weak three opening means, of course, that your partner must give you a little leeway when he is considering his response. As a general rule, I would suggest that the responder should disregard one of his tricks, or his first six high-card points, when he is contemplating raising his partner or making a jump response to a conventional take-out request: the overcaller will probably have based his intervention on the assumption that the opposite hand contained certain worthwhile values.

(*c*) Similarly, the defending side must always bear in mind that suits are likely to break badly once the opening bidder has shown a seven-card or longer suit. This is another reason for taking things fairly cautiously when your partner has managed to find a bid over the opponent's pre-emptive opening. In practice, I have found that pre-emptive bids often goad the opposition into overvaluing hands, whereas they should really err on the side of caution when there are long suits and bad breaks around.

There was a spectacular example of overvaluation of this kind in the 1981 'Varsity match between Oxford and Cambridge.

Dealer South; North–South vulnerable.

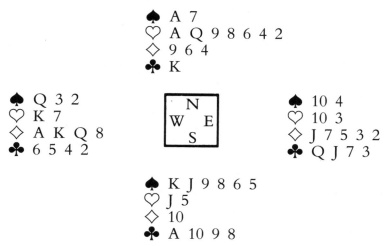

♠ A 7
♡ A Q 9 8 6 4 2
♢ 9 6 4
♣ K

♠ Q 3 2   ♠ 10 4
♡ K 7   ♡ 10 3
♢ A K Q 8   ♢ J 7 5 3 2
♣ 6 5 4 2   ♣ Q J 7 3

♠ K J 9 8 6 5
♡ J 5
♢ 10
♣ A 10 9 8

When Oxford University held the North–South cards, the bidding was as follows:

South	West	North	East
3♠	NB	4♠	NB
NB	NB		

West cashed one top diamond and switched to a club. Declarer won in dummy and played the ace, king and a third spade. The successful heart finesse and break now gave him 11 tricks: +650 to Oxford.

At the other table, the Oxford player in the West seat was convinced that he was being talked out of something:

South	West	North	East
3♠	Dble	4♠	NB
NB	Dble	NB	NB
NB			

In my view, one double was already more than enough on the West hand. The second one cost his team 8 imp, for the Cambridge University declarer had no difficulty in making an overtrick in his doubled contract and scoring +990.

THE JUMP OVERCALL

One aspect of competitive bidding on which I hold strong views is the meaning of a jump overcall. While the requirements laid down by the original Acol theorists were probably too stringent, I am absolutely certain that a jump overcall in a new suit is best used as a strength-showing bid. In my view, a jump overcall at the two-level should show a good six-card suit and the values for an opening bid. For example:

♠ K Q 10 9 7 4
♥ 7 3
♦ A 10 5
♣ K 8

Two spades is the best bid on this hand after an opening bid of one club, one diamond or one heart by your right-hand opponent. The solidity of the spade suit minimises the danger of running into a really damaging penalty double, and two spades has a potential preemptive effect as well as being a constructive move if your partner has good top cards and useful filling honours.

At the three-level, a jump overcall should show a slightly stronger hand, particularly when you are vulnerable. Perhaps:

♠ 7 4
♥ A J 3
♦ 10 4
♣ A K Q 10 7 4

After an opening bid of one diamond, one heart or one spade by your right-hand opponent, three clubs describes this hand quite well and should make it fairly easy for your side to reach any game contract which is available on your cards.

There is a disturbing modern tendency, particularly on the other side of the Atlantic, to favour weak jump overcalls. As well as placing too great a strain on the already overburdened take-out double, weak jump overcalls are feeble in a pre-emptive sense and give the opponents the option of making a penalty double or bidding on as if nothing had happened. Furthermore, they give a lot away about the distribution of the defenders' hands if, as is likely, the opening side still plays the final contract.

This last point is well illustrated by two hands played by Dr George Rosenkrantz, the inventor of the 'Pill' and an extremely successful bridge player, in the 1983 Bermuda Bowl Championships.

On the first hand, North dealt with North–South vulnerable.

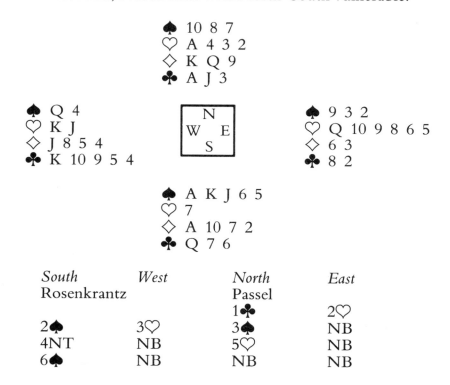

	♠ 10 8 7	
	♡ A 4 3 2	
	◇ K Q 9	
	♣ A J 3	

♠ Q 4		♠ 9 3 2
♡ K J		♡ Q 10 9 8 6 5
◇ J 8 5 4		◇ 6 3
♣ K 10 9 5 4		♣ 8 2

	♠ A K J 6 5	
	♡ 7	
	◇ A 10 7 2	
	♣ Q 7 6	

South	West	North	East
Rosenkrantz		Passel	
		1♣	2♡
2♠	3♡	3♣	NB
4NT	NB	5♡	NB
6♠	NB	NB	NB

West led the king of hearts against the final contract of six spades, and Rosenkrantz won with the ace and cashed the ace and king of spades, felling West's doubleton queen. He drew the outstanding trump, ruffed a heart in the closed hand and cashed three top diamonds. He now knew from the bidding and from the play so far that East's original distribution was 3–6–2–2, and he therefore threw West in with the jack of diamonds, forcing him to lead a club and concede three tricks in the suit.

George Rosenkrantz took similar advantage of information which he gained from the opponents' weak jump overcall to land another extremely thin slam on the following deal.

Dealer North; love all.

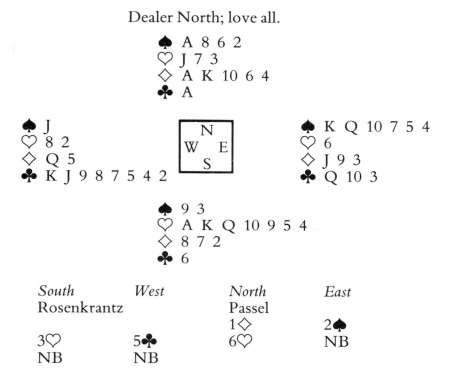

South	West	North	East
Rosenkrantz		Passel	
		1◇	2♠
3♡	5♣	6♡	NB
NB	NB		

West led the jack of spades against six hearts, and the fact that the defenders' spades were known to be 6–1 meant that there were strong possibilities of a successful avoidance play in diamonds. South won in dummy with the ace of spades, cashed the ace of clubs and crossed to hand with a trump to lead a small diamond towards dummy. When West played low, declarer went up with dummy's ace and crossed back to hand with a trump to lead a second diamond. When West produced the queen, South ducked to ensure the contract: the 3–2 diamond break meant that he could eventually discard his losing spade on dummy's long diamond, without East ever being able to gain the lead to cash a winning spade.

It would have made no difference if West had contributed the queen of diamonds on the first round of the suit: South would still have ducked the queen in order to establish dummy's long suit with perfect safety.

4   Some Passing Thoughts

People tell me that I have established quite a reputation over the years for not holding back in the bidding. Moreover, I am prepared to concede that this reputation may be justified, for I certainly believe that one has to be bold and courageous at the table in order to be a winning bridge player; in the long run, players who are excessively timid will win neither money nor Master Points.

Having said that, I like to think that, generally speaking, I only take chances in the bidding at opportune moments. My long years of experience at the game have given me sufficiently good judgement to be able to recognise the situations in which it pays to bid up a little, but that does not mean that I am not also able to pass when that appears to be the correct course of action. It is arguable that 'pass' is the most under-used bid in the bridge language. Most average players tend to bid far too frequently and I would like in this chapter to run through some of the most common situations in which it is tempting to make a positive bid but in which a good old-fashioned pass is likely to be the winning action.

BIDDING AFTER AN OPPONENT'S REDOUBLE
One common situation in which inexperienced players often bid when it is clearly correct to pass arises when their partner's take-out double has run into an immediate redouble from their right-hand opponent.

South	*West*	*North*	*East*
1◇	Dble	Redble	?

A pass by East in this position does *not* mean that he wants to defend against one diamond redoubled: it simply means that he has nothing worthwhile to contribute at this juncture, and his hand might be anything from a worthless holding like

Hand 1
♠ 7 4 2
♡ J 7 3
◇ 10 8 4
♣ 7 6 5 2

to a very promising holding like

Hand 2
♠ K 9 3
♡ A Q 7
◇ 7 6 4
♣ J 10 6 2

On Hand 2, East has such good values that he knows for certain that somebody at the table is not being completely honest. Since he has no way of showing this kind of hand immediately over the redouble, he does best to pass at his first turn and look for an opportunity to make a constructive move at a later stage.

As we have just seen, a pass over the opponent's redouble does not deny values. Conversely, of course, a positive bid over the redouble does not guarantee the possession of any high cards, for the doubler's partner might simply be expressing his view as to the correct denomination in which to play. Thus, if the bidding proceeds:

South	*West*	*North*	*East*
1◇	Dble	Redble	1♠

East might have either of the following hands:

Hand 3
♠ 7 6 5 4 3
♡ 8 6
♢ 9 7 4
♣ 10 6 5

Hand 4
♠ J 9 4 3
♡ 7 6 5
♢ 10 8 6 4 2
♣ 3

One spade is a very unattractive bid on Hand 4, but it is better for East to express a preference at this stage than to wait until his partner has been doubled in two clubs. However, Hand 4 is an exceptional case. In normal circumstances, there is no need for the doubler's partner to introduce a four-card suit once the redouble has relieved him of the obligation to bid. If East holds, for example

Hand 5
♠ J 9 4 3
♡ 7 6
♢ 6 3 2
♣ J 7 6 2

after the same auction, he can afford to bide his time and pass at his first turn. If West removes one diamond redoubled to one spade or two clubs, he should not be too disappointed with this dummy; and if he escapes to one heart, East can move on to one spade, implying that his spade holding is far from ideal and that he has a little something by way of support for clubs.

BIDDING IN THIRD POSITION

For tactical reasons, it is sometimes correct to open the bidding on sub-minimum values when you are the third to speak and the first two players have passed. It is generally true to say that the opponents will be able to bid more accurately if they are given a clear run than if they have to cope with an opening bid against them, and I am all in favour of opening light if I have a worthwhile suit. For example:

North
- ♠ K Q J 7 3
- ♡ 9 6 4
- ♢ A 9 2
- ♣ 4 3

If South and West both pass originally, my view is that North should open one spade on the above hand at any vulnerability. There are three arguments in favour of this course of action. First, the pre-emptive effect of the spade suit is such that one spade will deprive the opponents of almost a complete round of bidding. Second, North's spades are so good that he certainly wants South to lead the suit if East eventually becomes the declarer. And finally, an opening bid of one spade may make it difficult for the opponents to play in no trumps even if that is their best spot: if East was planning to open the bidding with 1NT, for example, he will have to think again if North gets in first with one spade.

Suppose that we now reshuffle the North hand slightly:

- ♠ Q 7 4 3
- ♡ K 9 6
- ♢ A 9 2
- ♣ J 4 3

North has exactly the same number of high-card points, the same allocation of honour cards and the same intermediate cards as before, but I would not dream of opening in third position on this collection. There is now no suit worthy of mention and no suit which North particularly wants to be led, and my view is that players make far too many pointless opening bids simply because they are in third position. Once again, there is a great deal to be said for passing when you have nothing worthwhile to say.

Here is a typical example of what I consider to be a pointless third in hand opening. It occurred during the 1977 Guardian Easter Tournament, and it led to an excellent result for one of the country's most promising junior pairs at that time, M. Nardin and S. Lodge.

Dealer South; game all.

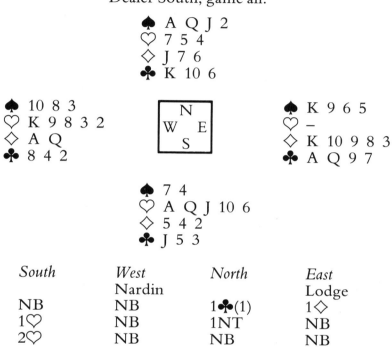

	South	West Nardin	North	East Lodge
	NB	NB	1♣(1)	1♦
	1♡	NB	1NT	NB
	2♡	NB	NB	NB

(1) This was a strange choice of opening bid. If North decides to make a light, third-in-hand opening, he might as well open one spade and pass whatever his partner responds. This would at least indicate where North's values lie for defensive purposes.

West led the two of clubs against two hearts. East won with the queen of clubs and switched to a small diamond. West cashed two top diamonds and returned a second club to his partner's ace. The king of diamonds allowed West to discard his remaining club, and East continued with a third round of clubs. West ruffed and switched to a small spade to the jack and king, and East returned the 13th club. South was forced to ruff high with the queen of hearts, and West ensured two more trump tricks for himself by refusing to over-ruff, discarding a small spade instead. When the smoke cleared, South had gone four down in his modest contract: 400 to East–West.

One of my own light opening bids worked out quite well during the 1975 European Championships in Brighton.

Dealer South; East–West vulnerable.

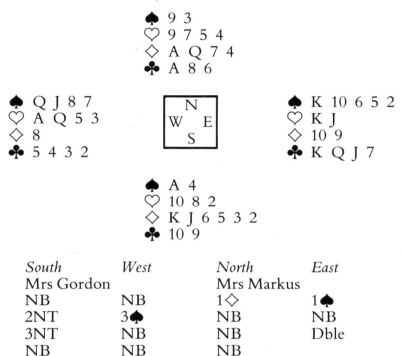

	♠ 9 3	
	♡ 9 7 5 4	
	◇ A Q 7 4	
	♣ A 8 6	
♠ Q J 8 7		♠ K 10 6 5 2
♡ A Q 5 3	N	♡ K J
◇ 8	W E	◇ 10 9
♣ 5 4 3 2	S	♣ K Q J 7
	♠ A 4	
	♡ 10 8 2	
	◇ K J 6 5 3 2	
	♣ 10 9	

South	West	North	East
Mrs Gordon		Mrs Markus	
NB	NB	1◇	1♠
2NT	3♠	NB	NB
3NT	NB	NB	Dble
NB	NB	NB	

Fritzi Gordon's bidding was quite justified. If I had a full-blooded opening bid, instead of a lead-directing third-in-hand effort, she could reasonably expect to have nine top tricks. Even as it was, she made the obvious eight tricks to lose 100 points and, since three spades was laydown for East–West, this was likely to be a winning board. In fact, it would take an opening club lead, or a diamond lead followed by a club switch, to defeat four spades, but we shall never know what would have happened to four spades. At the other table, North–South sacrificed in five diamonds, and Sandra Landy and Nicola Gardener (now Smith) collected a penalty of 500 – a swing of 9 imp to Britain.

IMMEDIATE SUIT OVERCALLS

Although defensive bidding is a vital part of the game, there is one crucial point in this connection which is all too often overlooked: the eventual declarer will find the hand easier to play if there has been opposition bidding than he will if the two defenders have remained completely silent throughout the auction. It follows from this that every overcall which you make must have a definite point to it, and must not be an example of what I call 'bidding for the sake of it'. To be a worthwhile venture, a suit overcall must fulfil at least one of the following criteria:

(*a*) It must have a pre-emptive effect. Overcalls in the suit ranking immediately below the opener's are particularly advantageous in this context: for example, one spade over one club, two diamonds over one heart etc.

(*b*) It must indicate the best lead to a partner who is likely to be on lead and who will otherwise be completely in the dark.

(*c*) It must be a constructive attempt to reach a playable contract for the defending side.

(*d*) It must be a first move towards finding a possible sacrifice if the opening side pushes on to game. A typical overcall which falls under this heading would be one spade over one heart at favourable vulnerability.

If you are contemplating an overcall which does not meet any of these conditions, my advice is simple. Do not do it. Pass. To bid for the sake of it can only help the opponents. Two hands should serve to emphasise this important point.

♠ K J 9 6 3
♡ Q 4
♢ Q 7 2
♣ A 10 5

North–South vulnerable.

South	West	North	East
1♣	?		

In this situation, West has everything to gain by overcalling. In fact, a bid of one spade over one club meets all four of the criteria which I have set out here, for it has a good pre-emptive effect, it might indicate the best lead to partner if North eventually becomes the declarer, it might be the first move towards locating the correct contract if the hand belongs to East–West, and it might indicate a possible sacrifice if the hand belongs to North–South.

And now, the same hand in a slightly different order.

♠ Q 4
♥ Q 7 2
♦ K J 9 6 3
♣ A 10 5

East–West vulnerable.

South	West	North	East
			NB
1♣	?		

An overcall of one diamond would be almost pointless. It has absolutely no pre-emptive effect; it is most unlikely that the hand belongs to East–West in view of East's original pass and West's poor holdings in the major suits; and East–West will almost never want to sacrifice in five diamonds at adverse vulnerability. The only possible benefit to be derived from an overcall in this position is that it might persuade your partner to lead a diamond if North eventually becomes the declarer, but it is important not to overstate the point. It is to be hoped that if the bidding were to proceed, say

South	West	North	East
			NB
1♣	NB	1♥	NB
2♣	NB	3NT	NB
NB	NB		

East might have the wit to lead a diamond rather than a spade from a holding of ♠J–x–x–x–x plus an outside jack.

One example from actual play will serve to illustrate the way in which an expert declarer can utilise the information which he has derived from an overcall in order to land an extremely tricky contract.

Dealer South; game all.

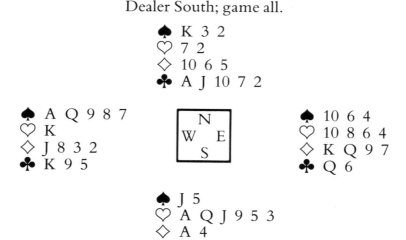

```
              ♠ K 3 2
              ♡ 7 2
              ◇ 10 6 5
              ♣ A J 10 7 2

♠ A Q 9 8 7        N         ♠ 10 6 4
♡ K            W       E     ♡ 10 8 6 4
◇ J 8 3 2          S         ◇ K Q 9 7
♣ K 9 5                      ♣ Q 6

              ♠ J 5
              ♡ A Q J 9 5 3
              ◇ A 4
              ♣ 8 4 3
```

South was the late Leslie Dodds, one of the great gentlemen of bridge and one of the few players whom it was as much a pleasure to play against as with. He opened one heart and ended up in the pushy contract of four hearts after West had overcalled one spade and North had overbid. West led the 2 of diamonds to his partner's queen, and Dodds won with the ace and immediately finessed the 10 of clubs, losing to the queen. East cashed the king of diamonds and continued with a third round, and South ruffed and played the ace of hearts, felling West's singleton king. He then played a club to the jack and finessed the 9 of hearts to make an overtrick in a contract which would normally be defeated.

Leslie Dodds' reasoning was as follows. West must have had five spades for his overcall, and the lead and subsequent play marked him with J–x–x–x of diamonds. It had to be assumed if South was going to make his contract that West held the king of clubs, in which case his failure to insert the king on the first round suggested that he had three clubs. West was now placed with five spades, four diamonds and three clubs. He must therefore have a singleton heart and, since South could not afford to lose a trump trick, the contract could only be made if West's singleton was the king.

While I am not suggesting that West was wrong to overcall one spade on this hand, the story shows how revealing an overcall can be if the opening side eventually plays the hand. Unless you have a definite purpose in mind, therefore, do not overcall for the sake of it: pass and let the declarer find out the hard way about your distribution and your high-card strength.

RAISING OVERCALLS

We have just seen that the defending side should refrain from making an overcall if there is no demonstrable purpose behind the bid. Similar principles apply to raises of suit overcalls. The overcaller's partner should not raise the overcall unless he has a definite purpose in mind. For a raise to be worthwhile, it must fulfil at least one of the following conditions:

(*a*) It must have a pre-emptive effect. All jump raises are clearly pre-emptive, and certain single raises can also threaten to make life difficult for the opening side. For example:

South	West	North	East
1♣	1♢	1♡	2♢

East's raise to two diamonds in this sequence might make it difficult for North-South to locate a 4–4 spade fit: either North or South will have to have reversing values if a spade fit is to come to light. On the other hand:

South	West	North	East
1♣	1♢	1♠	2♢

East's bid of two diamonds in this sequence has little or no pre-emptive effect. If North–South have a spade fit, it has already been located; if they have a heart fit, North will be able to bid two hearts on the second round without showing substantial extra values.

(*b*) It must offer reasonable prospects of permitting the defending side to play the hand.

(*c*) It must pave the way towards a possible sacrifice bid at a later stage.

If your hand fails to meet any of these criteria when you are contemplating raising your partner's overcall, take my advice and pass. To make a pointless raise, another example of 'bidding for the sake of it', is losing bridge, for two reasons. First, the raise might assist the declarer in placing the cards and assessing the full distribution if the opponents eventually play the hand. Second, and more important, the raise might materially help the opponents in the bidding, in that they will be able to judge the situation better when they have a good fit. Here is a typical example of the way in which a pointless raise can backfire.

Dealer North; game all.

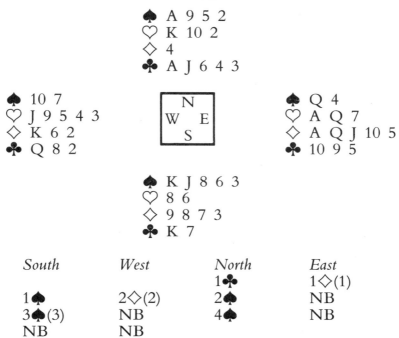

<pre>
                ♠ A 9 5 2
                ♡ K 10 2
                ◇ 4
                ♣ A J 6 4 3
♠ 10 7   ♠ Q 4
♡ J 9 5 4 3   ┌───────┐   ♡ A Q 7
◇ K 6 2   │   N   │   ◇ A Q J 10 5
♣ Q 8 2   │ W   E │   ♣ 10 9 5
                 │   S   │
                 └───────┘
                ♠ K J 8 6 3
                ♡ 8 6
                ◇ 9 8 7 3
                ♣ K 7
</pre>

South	West	North	East
		1♣	1◇(1)
1♠	2◇(2)	2♠	NB
3♣(3)	NB	4♠	NB
NB	NB		

(1) Although East's one diamond overcall has no pre-emptive effect, I certainly would not describe it as a pointless overcall. For all East knows at this stage, the hand may very well belong to his side.

(2) A pointless raise. Two diamonds has little or no pre-emptive effect; the hand can scarcely belong to East–West in view of East's simple overcall and in view of the fact that their principal weapon is a minor suit; and it is highly unlikely that East–West will be able to make a profitable sacrifice at game all.

(3) South would not normally consider making a try for game, but he knows that the king of clubs is a key card; more important, he knows that the North–South hands must fit well, now that West's raise to two diamonds has made it almost certain that North has at most one diamond.

POINT COUNT DOUBLES

One of the most common and expensive errors made by beginners and inexperienced players is what I call the 'point count double'. It is very easy to fall into the trap of basing all one's bidding on high-card points and drawing quite the wrong conclusion from the way in which the auction has developed. For example:

South	*West*	*North*	*East*
1♡	1♠	2♣	3♠

A beginner holding the South hand might well argue as follows. 'I have 14 points; my partner must have at least nine for his response at the two-level. This means that the opponents can only have 17 points at most, and there is no way in which they will be able to make nine tricks out of a possible 13. I shall therefore double three spades.' Experienced players realise that this argument is fallacious. The full deal on which the above auction was based could well be something like:

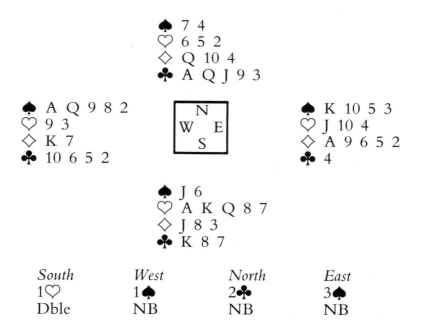

```
              ♠ 7 4
              ♡ 6 5 2
              ◇ Q 10 4
              ♣ A Q J 9 3
♠ A Q 9 8 2        N          ♠ K 10 5 3
♡ 9 3          W       E      ♡ J 10 4
◇ K 7              S          ◇ A 9 6 5 2
♣ 10 6 5 2                    ♣ 4
              ♠ J 6
              ♡ A K Q 8 7
              ◇ J 8 3
              ♣ K 8 7
```

South	*West*	*North*	*East*
1♡	1♠	2♣	3♠
Dble	NB	NB	NB

East–West have only 17 points in the two hands, and three of those are idle. However, West will have little difficulty in registering an overtrick in three spades doubled, and we can only hope that South will learn from this disaster and not fall into the same trap the next time the situation arises.

The ultimate illustration of the ineffectiveness of high-card points in certain situations is the classic Duke of Cumberland Hand. Some of you may not have heard the story attached to the following famous deal:

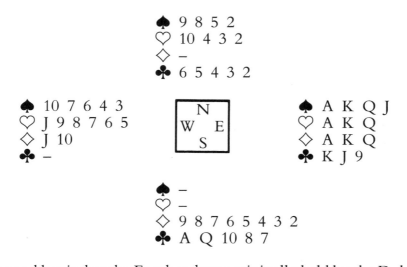

```
              ♠ 9 8 5 2
              ♡ 10 4 3 2
              ◇ –
              ♣ 6 5 4 3 2
♠ 10 7 6 4 3        N        ♠ A K Q J
♡ J 9 8 7 6 5    W     E     ♡ A K Q
◇ J 10              S        ◇ A K Q
♣ –                         ♣ K J 9
              ♠ –
              ♡ –
              ◇ 9 8 7 6 5 4 3 2
              ♣ A Q 10 8 7
```

Legend has it that the East hand was originally held by the Duke of Cumberland, the notorious son of George III. A crooked opponent who had dealt himself the South hand offered to bet that he could take all the tricks with clubs as trumps. The Duke, who was looking proudly at his 32-point hand, quite understandably doubted this could be done. He backed his opinion to the tune of £20,000 and some kibitzers to whom he showed the hand got in substantial side bets of their own. Of course, the Duke and his supporters were robbed. On any opening lead, even a trump from the East hand, South can establish the diamonds with three ruffs and pick up East's trumps by leading twice from dummy.

It would have been no use saying this to the Duke of Cumberland, but my golden rule in connection with penalty doubles is that you need tricks, not points. Going back to the earlier deal on which South doubled three spades, we find that his hand certainly did not meet this requirement. South cannot expect to make more than two heart tricks, and his length in clubs means that his partner's defensive prospects must be reduced. On this basis, therefore, South should not even consider doubling three spades: the only bid which he might contemplate is a gambling raise to four clubs, but I am certain that the best move is to pass.

Taking this argument one stage further, I have made another golden rule to the effect that, unless the opponents are clearly making a sacrifice bid, you should not make a penalty double of a suit contract without a trump trick or two. This is another reason why South should not have doubled three spades when he held

♠ J 6
♥ A K Q 8 7
♦ J 8 3
♣ K 8 7

Since the opponents have a 5–4 or better trump fit, J–6 is a very poor holding from a defender's point of view. It means that declarer will be able to draw trumps in two rounds and make at least seven trump tricks: five in the closed hand and at least two ruffs in dummy.

Here is one final example of the way in which a reliance on counting points can work out very poorly in a competitive auction. The following deal occurred during the Cannes Bridge Festival in 1978, when I was playing with John Collings, one of the most exciting players ever produced by this country.

Dealer West; love all.

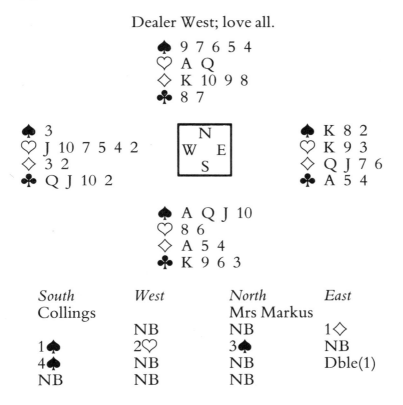

♠ 9 7 6 5 4
♡ A Q
◇ K 10 9 8
♣ 8 7

♠ 3
♡ J 10 7 5 4 2
◇ 3 2
♣ Q J 10 2

♠ K 8 2
♡ K 9 3
◇ Q J 7 6
♣ A 5 4

♠ A Q J 10
♡ 8 6
◇ A 5 4
♣ K 9 6 3

South	West	North	East
Collings		Mrs Markus	
	NB	NB	1◇
1♠	2♡	3♠	NB
4♠	NB	NB	Dble(1)
NB	NB	NB	

(1) 'I have 13 points, and my partner has bid at the two-level; South cannot possibly make ten tricks.'

In a sense, East was right. After an opening club lead, John Collings made 11. East had fallen into the trap of doubling without tricks and, since he was under the overcall, without a trump trick.

DOUBLING FORCING BIDS

Another example of bidding for the sake of it rather than making a disciplined and unrevealing pass occurs in connection with doubles of artificial, conventional and other forcing bids. For example, several players of my acquaintance can never resist doubling fourth-suit-forcing bids, and they fail to appreciate that such doubles can only help the opponents. In order to illustrate this point, let us consider the following auction:

South	West	North	East
1♣	NB	1♡	NB
1♠	NB	2♢	NB
?			

North's bid of the fourth suit asks the opener to describe his hand further, bidding 2NT or 3NT if he has a diamond guard, giving preference to hearts if he has three-card support or a doubleton honour, or otherwise doing the best he can. This can, of course, present quite a problem on certain South hands. For example:

♠ A Q J 4
♡ 3 2
♢ 5 4 3
♣ A K J 8

South has a good hand after his partner's forward-going move, but he has no way of describing it without distorting his holding quite considerably.

Now let us consider the same auction and assume that East feels constrained to double two diamonds, even though he has no compelling reason so to do:

South	West	North	East
1♣	NB	1♡	NB
1♠	NB	2♢	Dble
?			

South now has two additional bids at his disposal: redouble and pass. He can use a redouble to show a definite guard in diamonds, possibly A–x, but to suggest that it would be better if North played the no trump contract; and he can use a pass to show that he has nothing worthwhile to say at this stage. On the 15-point hand shown here, therefore, he can pass two diamonds doubled and leave it to his partner to make the next move. This next move might be, for example, for South to rebid his heart suit at the two-level, something which he could never do without the aid of East's impulsive double.

On the following deal, which was shown to me by my good friend Larry Gresh from Boulogne, West's double of a fourth-suit bid not only made the bidding easier for North–South, it also helped South to find the winning line of play in his eventual contract.

Dealer South; love all.

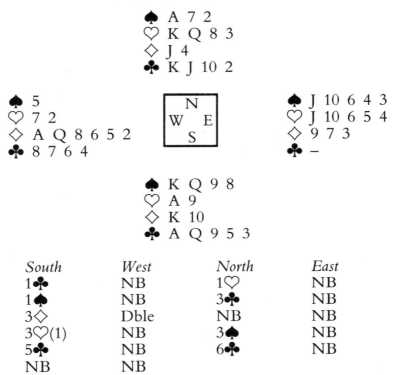

South	West	North	East
1♣	NB	1♡	NB
1♠	NB	3♣	NB
3♢	Dble	NB	NB
3♡(1)	NB	3♠	NB
5♣	NB	6♣	NB
NB	NB		

(1) Notice how West's impetuous double of three diamonds has effectively given South an extra round of bidding.

West led a trump against the final contract of six clubs, and East's void in clubs, coupled with West's double of three diamonds, gave declarer the clue to the winning play. He drew four rounds of trumps and cashed three rounds of hearts, discarding one of the diamonds from the closed hand. He then led a diamond to the king and ace, and West's diamond return, ruffed by declarer, squeezed East in the major suits. The moral of this hand is simple: silence is golden. Without West's revealing double of three diamonds, declarer would probably have played on diamonds, hoping that a fortunate guess would give him his 12th trick.

Just as a double of a fourth-suit-forcing bid has the effect of giving the opening side more room in which to manoeuvre, a double of a cue bid can also work to the detriment of the doubling side. One simple example will demonstrate why it is almost always correct to remain silent while the opponents are engaged in conversation:

South	West	North	East
1♡	NB	1♠	NB
3♣	NB	4♣	Dble

North's bid of four clubs is obviously a cue bid. This being the case, East's premature double, which is all too often based on something like ♣K–Q–10–x, can be of considerable benefit to North–South. It does, in fact, make two additional bids available to South: a redouble, which would show *second*-round control of clubs, and a pass, which would deny second-round club control and would also deny first-round control of diamonds, the next suit up. It may even be that East's double of four clubs will allow North to cue-bid both minor suit aces at the four-level, thus:

South	West	North	East
1♡	NB	1♠	NB
3♠	NB	4♣	Dble
NB	NB	4♢	

DOUBLING HIGH-LEVEL CONTRACTS

One final example of a situation in which inexperienced players do not pass as often as they should do is when their opponents have come to rest in a high-level contract which seems likely to go down. In such circumstances, it is only correct to double the final contract if you are 100 per cent certain of defeating it and if you are sure that the opponents will not be able to escape into an alternative contract which they might make. Here are two examples of ill-judged doubles which proved extremely costly. The first occurred in the Don Pepe Teams Tournament in 1977.

Dealer South; love all.

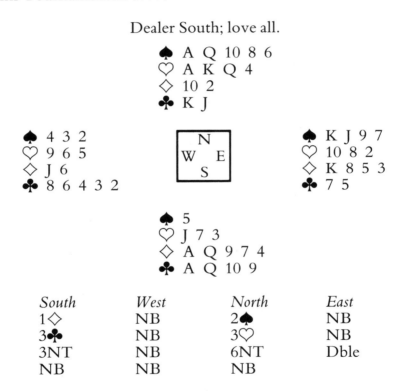

South	West	North	East
1♦	NB	2♠	NB
3♣	NB	3♡	NB
3NT	NB	6NT	Dble
NB	NB	NB	

South was Joel Tarlo, and he took full advantage of East's final double, which was obviously based upon a good holding in spades, to make his contract. West led the 3 of spades to the 10 and jack, and East switched to a small heart. South won in the closed hand and cashed four clubs and two more hearts, leaving the following position:

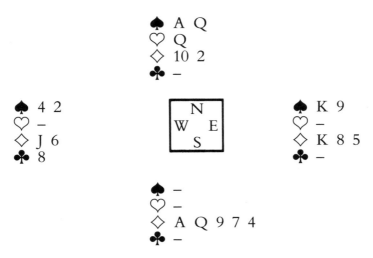

The last heart now squeezed East, who was forced to discard a diamond hoping that his partner held either the queen or J–x–x. Joel Tarlo was now able to take the remaining tricks by cashing the ace of spades and finessing the queen of diamonds. Without East's greedy double, South would probably be defeated in 6NT. His likely play would be to take two finesses in diamonds and fall back on the spade finesse when the diamonds fail to break.

My next hand occurred during a game of rubber bridge which I enjoyed at the British Embassy during my visit to the USA for the 1978 World Pairs Olympiad.

Dealer West; love all.

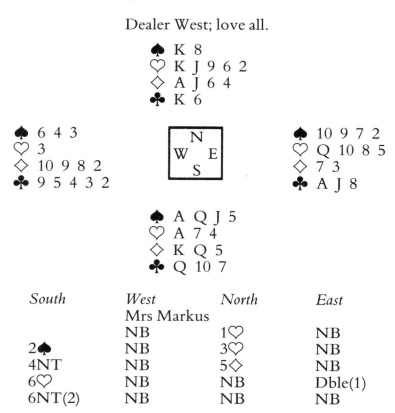

♠ K 8
♡ K J 9 6 2
♢ A J 6 4
♣ K 6

♠ 6 4 3
♡ 3
♢ 10 9 8 2
♣ 9 5 4 3 2

♠ 10 9 7 2
♡ Q 10 8 5
♢ 7 3
♣ A J 8

♠ A Q J 5
♡ A 7 4
♢ K Q 5
♣ Q 10 7

South	West	North	East
	Mrs Markus		
	NB	1♡	NB
2♠	NB	3♡	NB
4NT	NB	5♢	NB
6♡	NB	NB	Dble(1)
6NT(2)	NB	NB	NB

(1) My partner was later very sorry to have doubled six hearts. I assured him that he could not be blamed for doubling, although I am absolutely certain that it is correct to pass in such situations and collect as many 50s as are coming your way.

(2) Peter Jay, who was the British Ambassador at that time, took a good decision to convert to 6NT. He knew his right-hand opponent well enough to realise that he must have doubled six hearts on the strength of a certain trump trick plus the missing ace.

I led the 10 of diamonds against 6NT, and declarer cashed four diamonds and four spades to leave the following five-card end position:

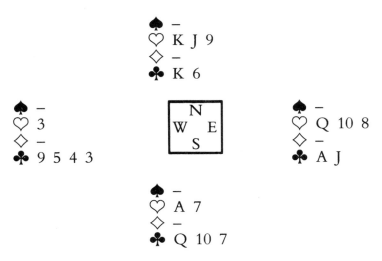

East had been forced to discard a club in order to retain three hearts, and a small club to dummy's king now gave the declarer the two club tricks which he required for his contract without even needing to take a finesse. Six hearts would, of course, have had absolutely no chance of making, and I am certain that East will be happy to pass and take the money if he is ever faced with this kind of situation again.

5   Two Different Worlds

I have always enjoyed playing rubber bridge, and one of my greatest regrets is that my current tournament commitments all over the world prevent me from playing as much of it as I would like. As a relaxation combined with mental exercise, there is nothing to beat a rubber between four players of a similar standard and playing for a stake just large enough to make everybody anxious not to lose.

Duplicate bridge, which is what I play nearly all the time these days, is in many ways a distorted version of the real game, for it makes each hand a completely separate entity and eliminates the exciting part-score battles which are such a feature of rubber bridge. On the other hand, of course, the fact that every pair in a tournament or both teams in a match play exactly the same hands makes duplicate bridge a good test of skill. The rubber bridge lament that 'I didn't hold a card all evening' would be an extremely feeble excuse for a poor performance at duplicate: if you and your partner averaged, say, 8 points per hand, then so did all the other pairs playing in your direction or so did the opponents who sat in your direction in a team of four match.

I am often asked by readers of my books and columns how they should vary their bidding tactics between rubber bridge and the duplicate game. On the whole, teams play and rubber bridge are fairly similar; the important distinction is between match-pointed pairs and rubber bridge, which are two completely different games and which call for two completely different approaches to bidding. In my estimation, the following are the principal areas of difference between bidding at rubber bridge, teams duplicate and pairs duplicate.

GAME BIDDING

Having said that rubber bridge and teams play are fairly similar, I have to start with one aspect of the game in which they differ widely: that of game bidding.

At teams play, the International Match Points scale offers disproportionate rewards for bidding and making game contracts. If you are vulnerable, for example, you stand to gain 10 imp by bidding a game which is not reached at the other table, whereas you will lose only 6 imp if you go one down in a game when your opponents linger in a part-score. Other things being equal, this means that it will pay you to have a shot at a vulnerable game if your chances of making it are 38 per cent or more. The rewards for non-vulnerable games are not so attractive, but you will still show a profit in the long run if you bid every non-vulnerable game which will make 46 per cent of the time.

The famous Italian Blue Team always took full advantage of the benefits to be derived from bidding thin games during their long spell of dominance in World and Olympic Championships. Here is a typical example of the marvellous pair of Garozzo and Belladonna in action.

Dealer West; North–South vulnerable.

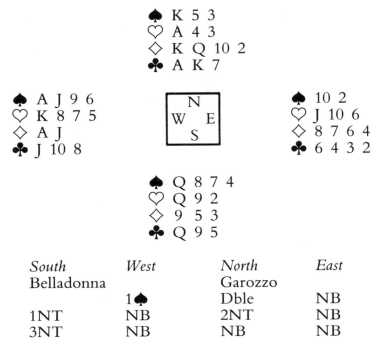

```
                    ♠ K 5 3
                    ♡ A 4 3
                    ◇ K Q 10 2
                    ♣ A K 7

   ♠ A J 9 6        ┌─────────┐        ♠ 10 2
   ♡ K 8 7 5        │    N    │        ♡ J 10 6
   ◇ A J            │  W   E  │        ◇ 8 7 6 4
   ♣ J 10 8         │    S    │        ♣ 6 4 3 2
                    └─────────┘

                    ♠ Q 8 7 4
                    ♡ Q 9 2
                    ◇ 9 5 3
                    ♣ Q 9 5
```

South	West	North	East
Belladonna		Garozzo	
	1♣	Dble	NB
1NT	NB	2NT	NB
3NT	NB	NB	NB

Looking at the North–South hands alone, 3NT would seem to be a poor contract. However, it is quite a good game to be in when all the opponents' high cards are concentrated in one defender's hand and when that defender has to make the opening lead.

West led a small heart, which ran to South's queen. Belladonna played a diamond to the jack and king, and a second diamond to the nine knocked out West's ace. The heart continuation lost to East's jack, and East cleared the suit, establishing a fourth trick for the defence. Having won with dummy's ace of hearts, however, Belladonna had only to knock out the ace of spades to make his contract: one spade, two hearts, three diamonds and three clubs.

It may appear as if the opening heart lead gave South his ninth trick, but in practice the contract is unbeatable, even on a club lead. Declarer plays on diamonds as before, and West eventually has to find two discards. Depending on what he hangs on to, he can be thrown in with a spade to give declarer an extra heart trick, or with a heart to concede an extra spade.

At the other table, the North American player in the South seat did not fancy his three queens, his balanced distribution and his lack of good intermediate cards. He therefore allowed his partner to play in 1NT, scoring three overtricks but losing 9 imp.

At rubber bridge, the odds are completely different, and you have to take into account a number of extraneous factors, such as how well your partner is likely to play the hand and how well your opponents are likely to defend. Generally speaking, it will pay you to have a shot at a close game when you are vulnerable; this is particularly true when your opponents are not vulnerable, for the odds will still be heavily in favour of your winning the rubber on the next hand or two even if you are defeated at your first attempt. When you are not vulnerable, however, you should only bid games which are odds-on chances, for the concealed value of a part-score is such that it should not be thrown away with reckless abandon.

At pairs play, the odds are fairly simple to assess: in a high-standard competition, you should bid any game which has a better than even chance of making, for you will thereby gain more often than you will lose. If the field is a little mixed, however, these odds do not quite hold good. Since there will probably be a number of pairs playing in the wrong denomination or in completely silly contracts, you will stand to achieve an over-average score by playing in a correct part-score; this means that you will need a slightly better than 51 per cent chance of making game before you jeopardise your safe part-score contract.

SLAM BIDDING

Small Slams

Generally speaking, your approach to bidding small slams should be the same at any form of scoring, in that it will pay to bid any slam which has a fractionally better than even chance of making. The only two provisos which I would like to make are first that you need considerably better odds when you are facing a poor partner at rubber bridge, when you will not want to tax him in the play and when you will be anxious to finish the rubber and cut again; and second that you need slightly better odds in an indifferent pairs event or in a match against an indifferent team, when you might well gain points merely by playing in the correct game contract.

Here are Italian stars Garozzo and Belladonna in World Championship action again, bidding a borderline vulnerable slam which appears at first sight to depend on a finesse. However, as so often happens, Belladonna was able to find a line of play which offered a better than 50 per cent chance.

Dealer South; North–South vulnerable.

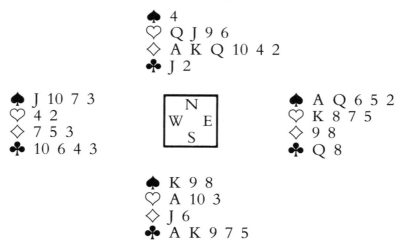

```
                    ♠ 4
                    ♡ Q J 9 6
                    ♢ A K Q 10 4 2
                    ♣ J 2
    ♠ J 10 7 3            N           ♠ A Q 6 5 2
    ♡ 4 2            W         E      ♡ K 8 7 5
    ♢ 7 5 3               S          ♢ 9 8
    ♣ 10 6 4 3                        ♣ Q 8
                    ♠ K 9 8
                    ♡ A 10 3
                    ♢ J 6
                    ♣ A K 9 7 5
```

South	West	North	East
Belladonna		Garozzo	
1NT(1)	NB	2♣(2)	NB
2◇(3)	NB	3♣(4)	NB
3◇(5)	NB	3♡(6)	NB
3NT(7)	NB	4◇	NB
4♡(8)	NB	4♠	NB
4NT(9)	NB	5◇	NB
6♣	NB	6◇	NB
NB	NB		

(1) I have 13–15 points and a balanced hand.
(2) Have you a four-card major suit?
(3) No.
(4) Tell me more about your distribution.
(5) I have a five-card minor suit.
(6) Really? Which one?
(7) Clubs.
(8) I have the ace of hearts.
(9) I have a very suitable hand for a slam.

West led the jack of spades against six diamonds, and East won with the ace and switched to the eight of clubs. South won with the ace, drew trumps in three rounds and led the jack of clubs to the queen and king. He now led the nine of clubs, and the moment of truth arrived when West played low. He could ruff in dummy in the hope of bringing down the ten of clubs from East or finding the king of hearts well-placed. Or he could run the nine of clubs, disposing of all the heart losers in dummy if the ruffing finesse succeeded. This was only one chance against two, but Belladonna thought it extremely unlikely that East would have switched to a club from an original holding of Q–10–8. He therefore discarded a heart from dummy to make the slam, only to find that the heart finesse was right all the time.

At the other table, the North American North–South pair languished in 3NT, as I fear you and I might also do, and that was a further 12 imp to the great Italian champions.

Grand Slams

Players are understandably extremely cautious about bidding grand slams at rubber bridge. In purely mathematical terms, however, a grand slam is a good investment as long as it will make twice in three times, and this means that a grand slam which depends at worst on a 3–2 break in a key suit is just about worthwhile.

At teams play, the vagaries of the imp scale are such that you do not need quite such good odds before you have a shot at seven; a grand slam which has a 57 per cent chance of success is a reasonable investment.

It is at match-pointed pairs that the assessment of whether or not it will pay to have a shot at a grand slam becomes a complex one. In pure theory, a grand slam which has a 51 per cent chance represents a worthwhile gamble, for you will gain match points more often than you will lose them. This assumes, however, that the field with whom you are comparing will *all* bid the small slam, and this is very rarely true in practice. My experience suggests that one normally achieves a 70 per cent score simply by bidding a laydown six, for there is always somebody playing the wrong denomination or chickening out at the crucial point. This means that you are almost certainly jeopardising an over-average score by pushing on to seven, and I would suggest that, in practical play, you should look for the same 67 per cent odds which are required at the rubber bridge table.

SELECTING THE DENOMINATION

Selecting the denomination in which to play is comparatively straightforward at rubber bridge or teams, because your only aim should be to play in the *best* contract.

Things are quite different at match-pointed pairs, where the difference between +140 in three hearts and +130 in four clubs can be the difference between a top and an under-average score. In simple terms, your policy should be to avoid minor suit contracts as far as possible. This applies particularly at the game level, where you will so often find that an accurately-bid five clubs or five diamonds, scoring +400, turns out poorly because a proportion of the field contrives to make an overtrick in 3NT.

Of course, striving to play in the higher-scoring contracts, rather than the safe ones, often leads to some interesting and exciting battles between declarer and the defenders in match-pointed pairs competitions. Here is a typical example:

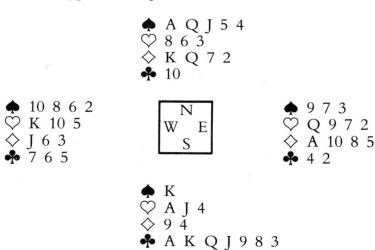

```
                    ♠ A Q J 5 4
                    ♡ 8 6 3
                    ◇ K Q 7 2
                    ♣ 10

  ♠ 10 8 6 2            N            ♠ 9 7 3
  ♡ K 10 5          W     E          ♡ Q 9 7 2
  ◇ J 6 3              S             ◇ A 10 8 5
  ♣ 7 6 5                            ♣ 4 2

                    ♠ K
                    ♡ A J 4
                    ◇ 9 4
                    ♣ A K Q J 9 8 3
```

As you will see, six clubs is unbeatable on the North–South cards. Striving for the top score in a pairs contest, however, South became the declarer in the inferior contract of 6NT, and West found the killing lead of a small heart. Declarer now had to resort to a 'stepping-stone' squeeze to land 12 tricks. He won the heart lead with the ace and cashed six rounds of clubs. West had to hold on to his four spades, or South would have been able to overtake the king of spades and make five spade tricks in dummy. West therefore discarded all his diamonds, leaving the following end position:

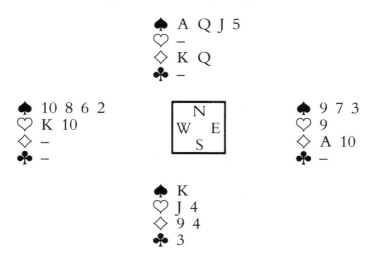

The last club now forced West to bare his king of hearts, and South read the situation correctly by cashing the king of spades and exiting with a heart, compelling West to win and provide access to dummy's three remaining spade tricks.

Declarer had to be able to read the end position exactly right, and it occurs to me that a deceptive defence might well defeat 6NT. The best counter is for the defender with four spades to discard two of them and for the defender with three spades to hang on to all three. On the actual layout, therefore, West should discard two spades and two diamonds, and East should discard three diamonds and two hearts. South might well then prefer to play East for an original 4–3–4–2 distribution, cashing the king of spades and exiting with a diamond in an attempt to achieve the 'stepping-stone' ending via the ace of diamonds, and going one down when East triumphantly produces another heart.

The need to avoid playing in minor suit contracts applies just as much at the part-score level as in games and slams, for nine tricks in a heart or spade contract will produce a better score than ten tricks in clubs or diamonds. On the following deal, the Austrian international player, Barbara Lindinger, even went to the lengths of playing in a suit which had been bid naturally by the opponents in order to avoid playing in a minor suit part-score. Barbara is the Head Teacher at a girls' college in Salzburg; in this respect, she is the Austrian equivalent of Britain's Sandra Landy and, as you will see, her declarer play also reaches a similar class.

Dealer West; game all.

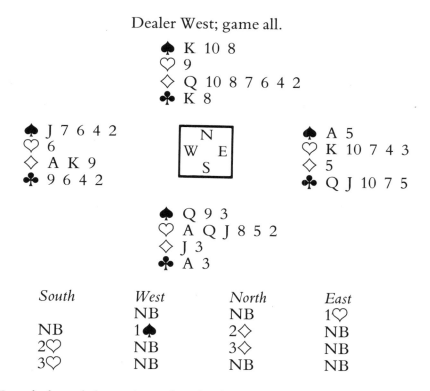

```
                 ♠ K 10 8
                 ♡ 9
                 ◇ Q 10 8 7 6 4 2
                 ♣ K 8
  ♠ J 7 6 4 2         N          ♠ A 5
  ♡ 6            W         E     ♡ K 10 7 4 3
  ◇ A K 9             S          ◇ 5
  ♣ 9 6 4 2                      ♣ Q J 10 7 5
                 ♠ Q 9 3
                 ♡ A Q J 8 5 2
                 ◇ J 3
                 ♣ A 3
```

South	West	North	East
	NB	NB	1♡
NB	1♠	2◇	NB
2♡	NB	3◇	NB
3♡	NB	NB	NB

West led a club against the final contract of three hearts, and declarer won with dummy's king and ran the 9 of hearts, which held the trick. A club to the ace was followed by a diamond, and West went in with the king and continued with another club. Declarer ruffed and led the queen of spades, which East correctly ducked. A second spade to the 10 drove out East's ace, and another club gave South her third trump trick. With the A–Q–J of trumps still intact, declarer was certain to make three more tricks: she exited with a spade, ruffed the club return and then exited with her last diamond. One spade, six hearts and two club tricks gave Barbara Lindinger nine tricks and a score of +140, beating all the other North–South pairs who scored +130 by making ten tricks in diamond part-scores.

SACRIFICE BIDS

Sacrifice bidding at rubber bridge must be kept to a minimum if you hope to be a long-term winner at the game. Unless it seems likely to be extremely cheap, it is certainly unwise to sacrifice at adverse vulnerability, for the odds will still be stacked heavily against your winning the rubber. Similarly, you should not pay too great a price to prevent the opponents achieving their first game when you are already vulnerable; even if they succeed in making their game contract, you are still in with a good chance of winning the rubber. The only situations in which you should seriously contemplate making a sacrifice bid are (a) at love all when you have a part-score to protect; and (b) at game all – but not if the opponents have a part-score towards their second game. Sacrifice bids should never cost more than 500, and they should be avoided if you are playing with the weakest player of the other three at the table and are not anxious to prolong the rubber.

At teams play, the mathematics of sacrifice bidding are much more straightforward, for it will clearly pay you to save if the penalty you incur is lower than the value of the opponents' game or slam. If the opponents are not vulnerable, therefore, it will pay you to concede −300 to save over their game; if they are about to make a vulnerable game, you can afford to go three down not vulnerable or two down vulnerable.

The situation is similar at match-pointed pairs, where each deal is once again a separate entity. The only piece of advice I would like to offer is that you should think twice about sacrificing over a slam bid against you at pairs. While it is perfectly true that to lose 900 in seven clubs doubled is better than losing 980 in six spades, it will not bring you in many more match points if few pairs have bid the slam. Unless the opponents have bid six with great confidence and absolutely no difficulty, therefore, you might be well advised to take your chances on defeating the slam rather than conceding 700 or more in a doubtful cause.

BIDDING ON PART-SCORE DEALS

The important concept to grasp when you first play in pairs competitions is that the size of your loss on a bad board may be immaterial. In other words, if you incur a large penalty on a part-score deal, it is unlikely to matter very much whether you lose 500, 800 or 1100; conversely, of course, you can earn yourself a zero by failing to make an overtrick in a game contract just as well as by going down in an impossible slam. At pairs play, it is the frequency of your gain or loss, rather than its size, which will determine the success or failure of your bidding tactics, and this is the argument I have heard advanced in support of one of my least favourite bidding devices: the weak no trump. Since its supporters argue that the 12–14 1NT can bring in two or three over-average boards for every large penalty which is incurred, they claim that it is an effective weapon at match-pointed pairs scoring. I do not completely agree with that argument, for reasons which I have set out in Chapter 3.

Furthermore, there is absolutely no case to be made for the weak no trump when you are vulnerable at teams or at rubber bridge, and I am pleased to say that my own favourite, the strong no trump, is still widely used by those who play the game for money. The auction on the following deal was in many ways typical of rubber bridge bidding.

Dealer North; love all.

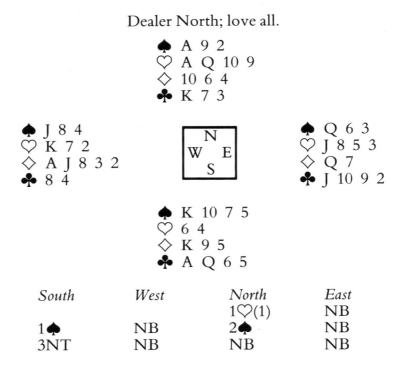

♠ A 9 2
♡ A Q 10 9
♢ 10 6 4
♣ K 7 3

♠ J 8 4
♡ K 7 2
♢ A J 8 3 2
♣ 8 4

♠ Q 6 3
♡ J 8 5 3
♢ Q 7
♣ J 10 9 2

♠ K 10 7 5
♡ 6 4
♢ K 9 5
♣ A Q 6 5

South	West	North	East
		1♡(1)	NB
1♠	NB	2♣	NB
3NT	NB	NB	NB

(1) As you will notice, North does not consider opening this modest hand with 1NT, even though he is not vulnerable. Tournament players would argue that an opening bid of one heart on this type of hand leaves you with an insoluble rebid problem after a response of two clubs or two diamonds, but rubber bridge players normally overcome this difficulty by using a non-jump rebid of 2NT on minimum balanced hands.

West led a small diamond against the natural contract of 3NT, and the declarer, George Lengyel, found the good shot of capturing East's queen with the king and playing a diamond straight back. West cashed his four diamond tricks, on which East discarded two hearts and a spade, and exited with a club. South won in the closed hand, successfully finessed the queen of hearts and cashed two more top clubs. The third club squeezed West in the majors and, since East was no longer able to guard either hearts or spades, Lengyel's ninth trick was bound to come either from the 10 of hearts in dummy or from the 10 of spades in the closed hand.

As you will see, no defence succeeds against this line of play. If West does not cash his diamond winners, South can finesse the 9 of hearts and develop three heart tricks; and if East discards differently, declarer can develop an additional trick in whichever suit East abandons completely.

We saw in the preceding deal that the key factor to be taken into account when you are considering any action at pairs is frequency: broadly speaking, if the bid which you are contemplating will succeed in improving your score more than 50 times in 100, it is worth doing – even though it may occasionally cost you a small fortune when it misfires.

The same is demonstrably not true at rubber bridge or imp scoring, when the *size* of any potential gain or loss is all-important, and this distinction should be borne in mind when you are considering whether or not to contest a part-score. At teams or rubber bridge, you should only get yourself embroiled in a part-score battle if your action is basically reasonably safe: that is, if you are most unlikely to lose more than 300 if things go wrong. At match-pointed pairs, on the other hand, you should try to compete for as many part-scores as possible, and Terence Reese once suggested that you should never allow the opponents to play where they want to play at the two-level.

The aggression which you must display if you want to succeed at pairs partly takes the form of risky overcalls, particularly in situations like 1♣–1♠, 1♢–2♣, 1♡–2♢ and 1♠–2♡ in which the overcall deprives the opponents of a lot of bidding space. More specifically, however, you need to be aggressive in the protective position: that is, when the opponents' bidding has petered out at a low level and you are the last to bid. In such circumstances, you must be prepared to take considerable risks in an effort to push the opponents a little higher or to locate a contract which would be profitable for your side.

Aggressive competition at pairs scoring does, of course, lead to a great deal of exciting bridge. Here, for example, is Bill Pencharz in action during the Philip Morris–Guardian Pairs Championship at the Guardian Easter Tournament in 1977.

East dealt at game all.

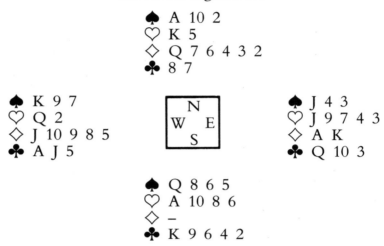

♠ A 10 2
♡ K 5
♢ Q 7 6 4 3 2
♣ 8 7

♠ K 9 7
♡ Q 2
♢ J 10 9 8 5
♣ A J 5

♠ J 4 3
♡ J 9 7 4 3
♢ A K
♣ Q 10 3

♠ Q 8 6 5
♡ A 10 8 6
♢ –
♣ K 9 6 4 2

When his opponents stopped in two hearts on the East–West cards, Pencharz bid a courageous three clubs on the South hand, hoping to push them one level higher. However, West was not to be tempted. He doubled and led the jack of diamonds. South ruffed, crossed to dummy with the king of hearts and ruffed another diamond. The ace of hearts and a heart ruff were followed by the queen of diamonds, ruffed by East with the 10 of clubs and over-ruffed with the king. Declarer now led his last heart, and West ruffed with the jack of clubs to leave the following six-card end position:

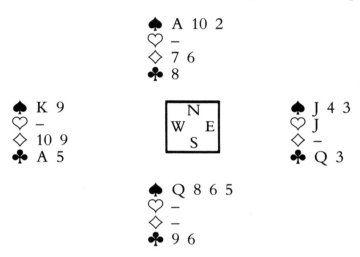

West now played the ace and another club, and East's jack of hearts became the defenders' fourth trick. However, East was now compelled to switch to a small spade and, when Pencharz guessed correctly by playing low from the closed hand and leading the 10 from dummy on the second round, he made the rest of the tricks and his doubled contract.

PENALTY DOUBLES

Game Contracts

The basic philosophy behind penalty doubles of freely-bid game contracts is the same at any form of scoring. Briefly, you should try to avoid what I call 'point count doubles': that is, doubles made solely because you have reason to suspect that the opponents do not hold the 25 or 26 points which are normally associated with a game contract. You need tricks, not points, in order to defeat their game, and I have found by experience that the really profitable penalty doubles occur not when the opponents are missing a certain number of points, but when their key suits are breaking badly. The time to double is when you can tell from your hand that the declarer is going to run into a nasty break or two and that the defenders' high cards are all well-placed – particularly when the auction has been something like

North	South		North	South
1NT	2♣	or	1♠	2♣
2♠	3♣		2♦	2♠
4♠			3♠	4♠

and you know that the opponents have very little, if anything, to spare.

Sacrifice Bids

At imp scoring or rubber bridge, your principal objective when you are confronted with what is clearly a sacrifice bid by your opponents should be to ensure a reasonable plus score. Since you stand to lose much more if you bid on and go down than you do if you double and take an inadequate penalty, it follows that you have to be pretty certain of success before you decide to accept the push rather than doubling the opponents' sacrifice bid and making certain of a reasonable plus score.

As is often the case, the problem is more difficult at match-pointed pairs, where you are likely to get just as bad a result from taking a 500 penalty from four spades doubled when you could have made +650 in hearts as you would from allowing yourself to be pushed overboard and going one down in five hearts. Once again the all-important question at pairs scoring is that of frequency: if you think it unlikely that you will collect more than 500 from four spades doubled, you should push on to five hearts whenever you believe that you will make 11 tricks more than 50 per cent of the time.

Part-Scores

It is in connection with penalty doubles of part-scores that you will find that the recommended tactics vary most between the three types of bridge. If the doubled part-score would be enough to give the opponents game, it is not wise to take any risks at rubber bridge or teams; in that situation, you should only make a penalty double if all the evidence suggests that the contract is likely to go two down.

Playing match-pointed pairs, on the other hand, you should adopt a much more aggressive approach to low-level penalty doubles. There are many situations, for example, in which you have every reason to believe that the opponents may have overstepped the mark in an effort to muddy your bidding waters and that the layout of the cards is such that they are in for a rough passage. If that is so, you should double them. Provided that your judgement is more or less correct and you collect a number of 200, 300 and 500 penalties on part-score deals, you can afford to lose the occasional 470 or 670 and still show a substantial gain on the exercise.

There is a far more important situation in which you simply have to be quick on the trigger at match-pointed pairs. This arises when it is clear to everybody at the table that the opponents are trying to steal your part-score. Consider an auction of this kind:

South	West	North	East
	NB	1♡	NB
2♡	NB	NB	2♠
3♡	3♠	NB	NB
?			

If South was correct to try to play in first two hearts and then three hearts, it seems likely that the travelling scoresheet will show a number of +140s in the North–South column. Not everybody will encounter such determined competition from East–West, and this means that to defeat them in three spades and collect, say, +100 is likely to lead to a considerably below-average score. If South has the slightest excuse in terms of defensive values, therefore, his only hope is to double three spades and try to collect 200 or 300, depending on the vulnerability.

Many players I know would be very reluctant to make a risky double in the above situation, 'in case they made it'. My answer to this would be that −530 or −730 in three spades doubled is only a bottom, and that South would be most unlikely to score very many match points for losing −140 on the board: if the opponents, who have passed originally, succeed in bidding and making three spades, they will probably achieve, and deserve, a top or near-top score.

Here is a hand from the Mixed Pairs Championship at the Juan-les-Pins Bridge Festival on which my partner, Leon Tintner, made a good match-pointed pairs double of a part-score contract.

Dealer East; North–South vulnerable.

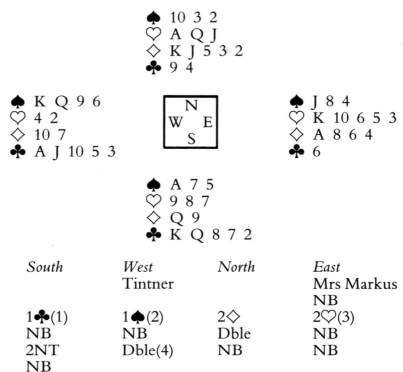

♠ 10 3 2
♡ A Q J
♢ K J 5 3 2
♣ 9 4

♠ K Q 9 6   ♠ J 8 4
♡ 4 2   ♡ K 10 6 5 3
♢ 10 7   ♢ A 8 6 4
♣ A J 10 5 3   ♣ 6

♠ A 7 5
♡ 9 8 7
♢ Q 9
♣ K Q 8 7 2

South	West Tintner	North	East Mrs Markus NB
1♣(1)	1♠(2)	2♢	2♡(3)
NB	NB	Dble	NB
2NT	Dble(4)	NB	NB
NB			

(1) The broken club suit and the six or seven side-suit losers made this a very dangerous opening bid at unfavourable vulnerability.

(2) A gallant attempt by my partner to prevent the opponents from finding their best fit.

(3) I should perhaps have bid two spades rather than two hearts, but I did not think that the bidding would stop there.

(4) A psychologically good double by my partner, who had assessed the position perfectly. He realised that to collect +100 from 2NT would be a bad score if other East–West pairs were making a part-score in hearts or spades; he also realised that to concede −120 if 2NT made would probably give us a bad score in any case, and that it would not cost us very many match-points if we lost 690 in 2NT doubled rather than 120 in 2NT undoubled.

West led the 4 of hearts, and I allowed dummy's jack to win the first trick, playing an encouraging 6. Declarer played a diamond to the queen and a second diamond to dummy's king, and I won with the ace and switched to a small spade, which declarer ducked to my partner's queen. West continued with his remaining heart, and South went up with dummy's ace, on which I dropped the 10, and attempted to cash the diamonds. When he discovered the bad break, he switched his attention to the club suit. West captured the king of clubs with the ace and, in response to my suit-preference signal with the 10 of hearts, returned the king of spades. Declarer was now doomed. He could have escaped for one off by ducking the king of spades, winning the next spade and exiting with a small club to end-play West. At the table, however, the end position was far from clear, and South went two down to give us the excellent score of +500 on a part-score board.

COMPETITIVE DOUBLES

Despite what I said in the previous paragraph about the need to make more tight penalty doubles of part-score contracts at pairs, the tendency among experienced match-pointed pairs players is actually to have fewer doubles available for use in a punitive sense. I am not a great believer in non-penalty doubles myself, but I know from experience that a number of very good players have some or all of the following competitive doubles in their armoury:

	South	*West*	*North*	*East*
(a)	1♣	1♠	Dble	

The Sputnik or negative double, suggesting a four-card heart suit and an inability to bid at the two-level.

	South	*West*	*North*	*East*
(b)				1♣
	1♦	1♠	Dble	

A competitive double, showing tolerance for diamonds and a five-card heart suit.

	South	*West*	*North*	*East*
(c)			1♠	2♡
	2♠	3♡	Dble	

A game-try double. Notice that North has no space available in which to make a normal trial bid.

	South	*West*	*North*	*East*
(d)				1♠
	Dble	2♠	Dble	

A responsive double, showing the values to compete and suggesting that South should select the denomination.

All the above doubles would probably be construed as penalty doubles at the rubber bridge table. In fact, apart from straightforward take-out doubles immediately over opening bids, very few doubles are not penalty doubles in the money game. I was reminded of this point by a hand from the House of Commons versus House of Lords match in 1981.

```
                    ♠ Q 9
                    ♡ J 9 7 4 2
                    ◇ J 7 5
                    ♣ K J 2
  ♠ A K J 8 7 4 2      ┌─────────┐      ♠ 10 5 3
  ♡ 8 6                │    N    │      ♡ Q 5 3
  ◇ 9 4                │  W   E  │      ◇ 8 6 2
  ♣ A 6                │    S    │      ♣ 9 8 7 5
                       └─────────┘
                    ♠ 6
                    ♡ A K 10
                    ◇ A K Q 10 3
                    ♣ Q 10 4 3
```

When the House of Lords pair, the Duke of Marlborough and the
Earl of Birkenhead, held the North–South cards, they reached the
second-best game contract of five diamonds; however, all was well
when the heart finesse succeeded.

At the other table in the match, Lord Lever displayed his usual
impeccable judgement by making a pre-emptive overcall on a hand
which would normally be considered too strong for such a manoeuvre.

South	West	North	East
1◇	3♠	NB	NB
NB			

Three spades went one down, and West had succeeded in talking his
opponents out of their game contract while restricting his own losses
to a minimum.

This hand illustrates the big difference between rubber bridge and
duplicate. The Parliamentarians are all rubber bridge players, and
they tend to regard all doubles as penalty doubles. Tournament
players, on the other hand, use a number of doubles as take-out
manoeuvres, and this would apply in the re-opening position described above. In my view, the full auction on the above deal should
proceed as follows:

South	West	North	East
1◇	3♠	NB	NB
Dble	NB	4♡	NB
NB	NB		

PLAY

6 Stop, Look and Listen

Most complex squeezes and end-plays can be planned only after the declarer has found out quite a lot about the distribution of the adverse hands, and about the whereabouts of the missing high cards. On the vast majority of hands, however, declarer will be able to map out his line of play fairly comprehensively when he first sees dummy, and the fate of a great many contracts will depend on the accuracy of declarer's planning at trick one.

I strongly recommend that, whenever you are playing a hand, you take your time before proceeding with the first trick. Over the many years during which I have played bridge at various levels, I have developed a routine which concentrates my attention on the key points which I should be considering before I embark on the play of any hand. After studying dummy and the opening lead, I quickly ask myself the following questions:

1 Have I enough winners to give me my contract?
2 Am I in danger of losing too many tricks?
3 Are there any problems of communications or entries?
4 What have I found out from the opponents' bidding?
5 What have I found out from the opening lead?
6 What can go wrong?

In the hope that you might be persuaded to adopt this kind of approach whenever you become the declarer, I would now like to go through these six key points in a little more detail.

HAVE I ENOUGH WINNERS TO GIVE ME MY CONTRACT?

When you are counting your winners at the start of a hand, you will find that you have a number of certain winners plus a number of additional winners which you might be able to develop during the play. The number of additional winners which you require in order to make your contract is the key figure, for this will determine (a) which suit you should play on; (b) the way in which you should play that suit; and/or (c) the way in which you should play other suits.

Here is a deal from rubber bridge on which the declarer committed the cardinal offence of failing to count his tricks.

Dealer South; game all.

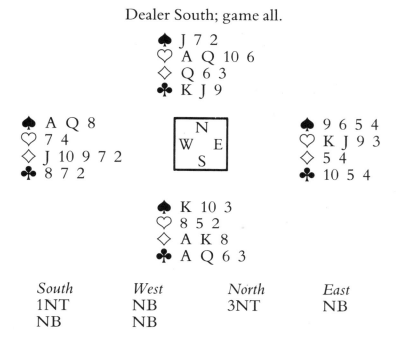

♠ J 7 2
♡ A Q 10 6
◇ Q 6 3
♣ K J 9

♠ A Q 8
♡ 7 4
◇ J 10 9 7 2
♣ 8 7 2

♠ 9 6 5 4
♡ K J 9 3
◇ 5 4
♣ 10 5 4

♠ K 10 3
♡ 8 5 2
◇ A K 8
♣ A Q 6 3

South	West	North	East
1NT	NB	3NT	NB
NB	NB		

West led the jack of diamonds against 3NT, and South won in the closed hand and immediately played a heart to dummy's 10. East won with the jack and returned his second diamond, and declarer went up with the ace and finessed the queen of hearts. When this lost to the king, declarer was in trouble. East switched to a spade, and West won with the queen and knocked out dummy's queen of diamonds, leaving South with the eight tricks with which he had started. South then cashed four rounds of clubs and the ace of hearts, hoping that the hearts would divide 3–3. When East was revealed to hold four hearts, all that was left for South was to play a second spade, but West won with the ace and cashed an established diamond. South had therefore gone down in 3NT despite a combined point-count of 29.

South bemoaned his bad luck in finding both the hearts and both the spades wrong, but he had only himself to blame. After the opening diamond lead, he could count eight certain tricks. All he had to do, therefore, was to lead a spade at trick two; nothing could then have prevented him from developing a spade as the vital ninth trick.

AM I IN DANGER OF LOSING TOO MANY TRICKS?

Every expert has his own way of planning the play at trick one, but it is fairly common to concentrate on one's winners in a no trump contract and on one's losers in a suit contract. It is certainly true that the number of established or potential losers in a suit contract will often determine the order of priority in which you should tackle the various tasks with which you are faced. Here is an example of what I mean, again from rubber bridge.

Dealer East; North–South vulnerable.

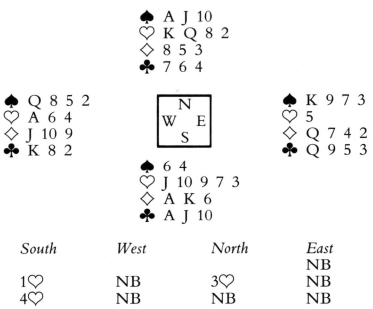

♠ A J 10
♡ K Q 8 2
♢ 8 5 3
♣ 7 6 4

♠ Q 8 5 2   ♠ K 9 7 3
♡ A 6 4   ♡ 5
♢ J 10 9   ♢ Q 7 4 2
♣ K 8 2   ♣ Q 9 5 3

♠ 6 4
♡ J 10 9 7 3
♢ A K 6
♣ A J 10

South	West	North	East
			NB
1♡	NB	3♡	NB
4♡	NB	NB	NB

After the lead of the jack of diamonds, a preliminary count of winners reveals that there are eight certain tricks: four hearts, two diamonds and two black suit aces. The two additional tricks which South needs must take the form of one spade and one club; he therefore plans to take two finesses in both black suits and to rely on finding at least one high honour well placed in each case.

So much for winners. Moving on to count his losers, declarer finds that, as things stand at trick one, he is in danger of losing four tricks: one spade, one heart, one diamond and at least one club. The only chance of avoiding one of these is to discard a diamond from the closed hand on one of dummy's spades, and South should realise that this project requires his urgent attention. If, for example, he were to begin the play of the hand by starting to draw trumps, the defenders would win the ace of hearts and knock out South's second diamond guard, thereby establishing four certain tricks for themselves.

This count of losers points the way to the correct sequence of play. South must win the first round of diamonds and finesse the 10 of spades. East wins and returns a second diamond, and declarer wins in the closed hand and takes a second spade finesse. When the jack holds, he discards his losing diamond on the ace of spades before embarking on the trumps. He subsequently uses the heart entries to dummy in order to take two club finesses, and the fact that the club honours are split means that he is able to land his vulnerable game.

The order of play described here represents the only legitimate hope of ten tricks, and it is important to follow the thought processes which lie behind it. It is interesting to note, however, that West can thwart the declarer if he makes the brilliant play of inserting the queen on the first round of spades: declarer has to win with dummy's ace, and the absence of a quick entry to dummy now means that the defenders will be able to establish and cash their diamond trick before South can find a home for his loser in the suit.

ARE THERE ANY PROBLEMS OF COMMUNICATIONS OR ENTRIES?

The preliminary count of winners and losers will determine the suit(s) on which you have to play in an attempt to make your contract, and you may have to conserve your entries so that you can be sure of being in the right place at the right time.

As well as making sure that the communications between your own two hands are satisfactory, your planning at the first trick should include a brief consideration of the defenders' comings and goings. It may be, for example, that you can make the defenders' task much more difficult by ducking the opening lead. A little forethought by the declarer would certainly be well rewarded on the following deal, which I came across in *The Country Life Book of Bridge Play Technique*, an interesting book by Pat Cotter and Derek Rimington.

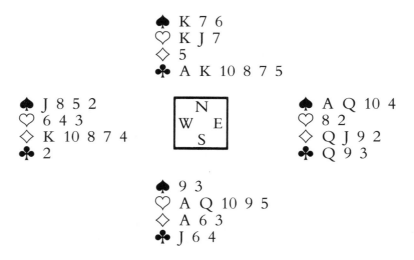

♠ K 7 6
♡ K J 7
◇ 5
♣ A K 10 8 7 5

♠ J 8 5 2   ♠ A Q 10 4
♡ 6 4 3   ♡ 8 2
◇ K 10 8 7 4   ◇ Q J 9 2
♣ 2   ♣ Q 9 3

♠ 9 3
♡ A Q 10 9 5
◇ A 6 3
♣ J 6 4

West leads a small diamond to his partner's jack against the natural contract of four hearts. If South wins the first diamond and ruffs a diamond in dummy, he can cross back to the closed hand with a trump in order to ruff his last diamond. Now, however, he cannot get back to hand in order to draw the outstanding trumps, and he will probably rely on the clubs being 2–2 and go one down when they are not.

The safest play for ten tricks is to allow East's jack of diamonds to hold the first trick! No return by East can damage declarer. If he returns a trump or a diamond, South can cash the ace of diamonds, ruff a diamond, draw trumps in three rounds and run the jack of clubs – safe in the knowledge that East cannot do any harm if he gains the lead with the queen of clubs.

The following board occurred in the 1978 World Pairs Olympiad in New Orleans.

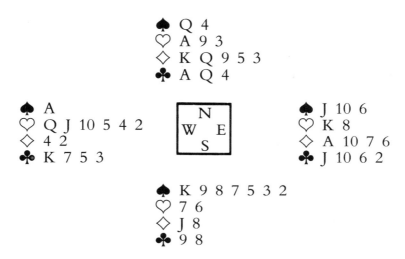

```
                    ♠ Q 4
                    ♡ A 9 3
                    ◇ K Q 9 5 3
                    ♣ A Q 4

 ♠ A                 ┌───────┐        ♠ J 10 6
 ♡ Q J 10 5 4 2      │   N   │        ♡ K 8
 ◇ 4 2               │ W   E │        ◇ A 10 7 6
 ♣ K 7 5 3           │   S   │        ♣ J 10 6 2
                     └───────┘
                    ♠ K 9 8 7 5 3 2
                    ♡ 7 6
                    ◇ J 8
                    ♣ 9 8
```

The normal contract was four spades, played by South. West led the queen of hearts to dummy's ace, and East unblocked by jettisoning the king. Declarer led a small diamond from dummy, and East went up with the ace and returned a second heart to his partner's 10. West continued with a third round of hearts, ruffed by East's 10 and over-ruffed by South's king. South now played a small trump towards dummy, and West won with the ace and continued with a fourth heart to promote East's jack of spades for the setting trick.

When Alan Sontag, the famous US champion, played the hand in four spades, he did his homework before playing to the first trick and realised that it might disrupt the defenders' communications if he ducked the queen of hearts lead. He won the second round of hearts with the ace and crossed to hand with the jack of diamonds in order to lead a small spade towards dummy, causing West's singleton ace to fan the air. There was no longer any way in which the defenders could establish a second trump trick.

Ducking the first round of hearts is a fairly automatic piece of good card-play technique; in this particular case, it was also the only way of making the game contract.

WHAT HAVE I FOUND OUT FROM THE OPPONENTS' BIDDING?

Although competitive bidding is an essential part of the game, it has one very serious disadvantage: if the opponents eventually become the declaring side, any competitive bidding which you have done will inevitably help the declarer to place the missing high cards and to form a general picture of the defenders' holdings.

As declarer, one of your first tasks before you play to the first trick should be to run through the bidding and remind yourself of what, if anything, you have learnt about the opponents' hands. South failed to do this on the following hand from the Harrogate regional final of the 1983 Sobranie Challenge Cup competition.

North
Dummy
♠ A 4
♡ 10 9 8 7 4
♢ A K
♣ K 9 6 5

South
♠ K 9 6 5
♡ K
♢ Q 10
♣ Q 10 8 7 3 2

West	North	East	South
1♣	Dble	NB	3♣
NB	3♡	NB	3NT
NB	NB	NB	

West led the 7 of spades against 3NT, and South captured East's jack with the king and immediately led a club to dummy's king. When East showed out, the contract was doomed and South realised too late what he had done wrong. Since West is marked on the bidding with the ace of clubs, the only possible 3–0 club break occurs when East is void: the contract is therefore assured provided that declarer wins the first trick with dummy's ace and leads a small club to the queen.

As well as gleaning vital information from the positive bids made by the opponents, it is also possible on occasions to deduce vital clues from their failure to bid. The following deal from rubber bridge is instructive.

Dealer West; love all.

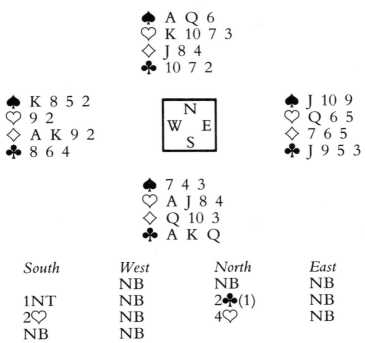

♠ A Q 6
♡ K 10 7 3
◇ J 8 4
♣ 10 7 2

♠ K 8 5 2
♡ 9 2
◇ A K 9 2
♣ 8 6 4

♠ J 10 9
♡ Q 6 5
◇ 7 6 5
♣ J 9 5 3

♠ 7 4 3
♡ A J 8 4
◇ Q 10 3
♣ A K Q

South	West	North	East
	NB	NB	NB
1NT	NB	2♣(1)	NB
2♡	NB	4♡	NB
NB	NB		

(1) Stayman, seeking a 4–4 heart fit in the hope that it would provide a better game contract than 3NT.

West led the ace of diamonds against four hearts, and South viewed dummy with some misgivings. He was certain to lose two diamonds and at least one spade trick. Even if he avoided a third-round diamond ruff, therefore, he would have to find the king of spades favourably placed *and* pick up the queen of trumps in order to make the contract.

Hoping for the best, South decided to plan the play on the assumption that the diamonds were either 4–3, or 5–2 and blocked, and that West held the king of spades. When declarer now reminded himself of what the auction had been, he succeeded in locating the queen of hearts without even playing a card. West had passed originally, and yet he was known to hold the ace and king of diamonds and was assumed to hold the king of spades. He was therefore most unlikely to hold the queen of trumps as well, for that would give him at least 12 points.

As you will see, South's careful thought before playing to the first trick paid handsome dividends. He won the third round of diamonds, drew trumps by playing to dummy's king of hearts and running the 10 on the second round, and subsequently took the spade finesse to land ten tricks.

WHAT HAVE I FOUND OUT FROM THE OPENING LEAD?

As well as the inferences about the distribution of the unseen high cards and unseen hands which declarer can derive from any bidding which the opponents have or have not done during the auction, there may also be some vital clues to be picked up from the opening lead.

Zia Mahmoud, the exciting Pakistani player who, I am pleased to say, spends quite a lot of his time in this country, certainly drew the correct inferences from the opening lead on the following deal. He then found a typically brilliant counter.

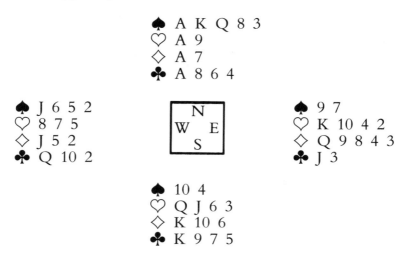

Zia reached the not unreasonable contract of six clubs, which appears at first sight to depend on a 3–2 club break and either a 3–3 spade break or the heart finesse. However, West made the contract appear considerably worse by finding the opening lead of the 8 of hearts, and the situation was now desperate.

Zia decided to take the lead at its face value and to assume that the king of hearts was off-side. He went up with dummy's ace of hearts, cashed the ace and king of clubs and made the remarkable play of running the 10 of spades. When this held the trick, declarer was home. He cashed four more spade tricks, discarding all his losing hearts, and the unfortunate West was not able to ruff until the fifth round – by which time all South's hearts had disappeared.

Notice that Zia's line of play was the only one to stand any chance of success. A 3–3 spade break would not have helped his cause, for he needed the defender who held three trumps to have to follow to *four* rounds of spades.

WHAT CAN GO WRONG?

One of my favourite bridge slogans has always been: 'Hope for the best, but provide for the worst'. With this in mind, I always find it worthwhile to pause before playing to the first trick and to ask myself what could possibly go wrong – and, more important, whether I can do anything about it if it does.

I enjoyed the following hand which I played with the Italian superstar Giorgio Belladonna at the 1981 Stratford-upon-Avon Congress. Praise from one of the greatest players of all time is praise indeed, and Giorgio was very complimentary about my performance on this occasion.

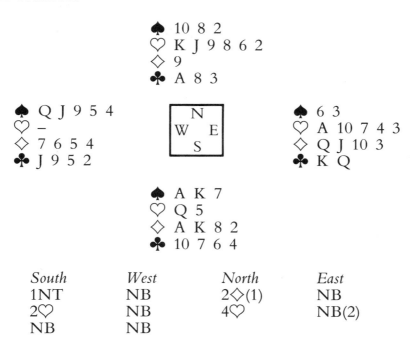

```
                    ♠ 10 8 2
                    ♡ K J 9 8 6 2
                    ◇ 9
                    ♣ A 8 3
  ♠ Q J 9 5 4      ┌─────────┐      ♠ 6 3
  ♡ —              │    N    │      ♡ A 10 7 4 3
  ◇ 7 6 5 4        │  W   E  │      ◇ Q J 10 3
  ♣ J 9 5 2        │    S    │      ♣ K Q
                   └─────────┘
                    ♠ A K 7
                    ♡ Q 5
                    ◇ A K 8 2
                    ♣ 10 7 6 4
```

South	West	North	East
1NT	NB	2◇(1)	NB
2♡	NB	4♡	NB(2)
NB	NB		

(1) A transfer bid, requesting me to bid two hearts.
(2) After a perceptible wriggle.

West led the queen of spades against the final contract of four hearts, and I paused to take stock. Provided that I did not lose two heart tricks, I could count ten winners and only three losers. The only thing which could go wrong was therefore a bad trump break and, in view of East's reactions during the bidding, I felt that it was quite likely that East would have length in trumps.

Having won the spade lead with the king, I led a small heart towards dummy, just in case West held the singleton ace. As I half expected, West showed out and dummy's king of hearts lost to East's ace. I won the spade continuation with the ace and cashed two top diamonds, discarding a spade from dummy. I then ruffed a diamond, crossed back to hand with the queen of hearts and ruffed another diamond, leaving the following position:

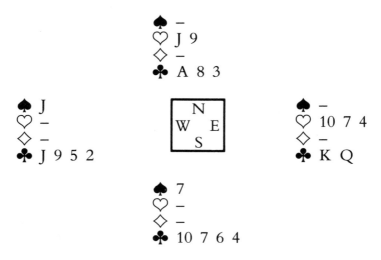

I had already made seven tricks, and when I now played the ace and another club, East was forced to win and return a trump to give me my contract.

Barnet Shenkin found a neat deceptive play in order to safeguard against things going wrong on the following deal from the Great Britain versus Sweden match during the 1979 European Championships in Lausanne.

Dealer East; love all.

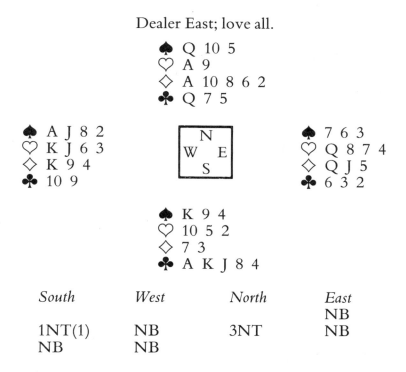

```
                    ♠ Q 10 5
                    ♡ A 9
                    ◇ A 10 8 6 2
                    ♣ Q 7 5

♠ A J 8 2            ┌─────────┐          ♠ 7 6 3
♡ K J 6 3           │    N    │          ♡ Q 8 7 4
◇ K 9 4             │  W   E  │          ◇ Q J 5
♣ 10 9              │    S    │          ♣ 6 3 2
                    └─────────┘
                    ♠ K 9 4
                    ♡ 10 5 2
                    ◇ 7 3
                    ♣ A K J 8 4
```

South	West	North	East
			NB
1NT(1)	NB	3NT	NB
NB	NB		

(1) Ostensibly showing 12–14 points and a balanced hand!

West led the 3 of hearts against 3NT and, assuming that the adverse hearts were divided 4–4, Shenkin realised that his contract depended on a successful guess in the spade suit: all that could go wrong was that South would misguess the position of the jack of spades and therefore fail to make the requisite two tricks in the suit.

Shenkin ducked the first heart in dummy and, when the queen appeared from East, false-carded by playing the 5 of hearts from the closed hand. East returned the 4 of hearts to dummy's ace, and declarer contributed the 10 in an attempt to persuade the defenders that he had a doubleton heart in each hand. The deception worked, for West unblocked the jack on the second round of hearts, clearly playing his partner for a five-card heart suit. Shenkin now cashed his five club tricks, on which West discarded one diamond and two spades, and led a small spade towards dummy. Just as Shenkin had planned, West hopped up with the ace in the hope of cashing three more heart tricks. He must have been extremely disappointed when the 2 of hearts finally appeared from the South hand.

7   A Walk on the Embankment

Beginners and inexperienced players are often in far too much of a hurry to draw trumps. In the back of their minds, no doubt, they recall cautionary tales of players from the London Clubs who, having failed to draw trumps and having had their side-suit aces and kings ruffed by small cards, have been forced to spend the night walking on the Embankment, penniless and footsore.

In reality, it is very often correct *not* to draw trumps immediately. Those of you who have watched expert players at the wheel will no doubt have noticed that to draw the opponents' trumps is their top priority on only about half the hands – the remaining 50 per cent of the time, the skilled declarer will deem it necessary to concentrate his attention first on some other aspect of the play.

It will probably be helpful if I set out in this chapter a number of reasons why it may be the correct play to delay drawing trumps. The declarer should not attempt to extract the opponents' teeth immediately in the following circumstances:

IF HE HAS TO ARRANGE FOR THE DISPOSAL OF A SIDE-SUIT LOSER FIRST

I always recommend that the declarer in a suit contract should count his losers as well as his potential tricks when he first plans the play. If this preliminary count indicates that there is a danger of the contract going down at a fairly early stage, some urgent remedial action may be required. Furthermore, this action may need to be taken *before* trumps are played, particularly if the opponents are likely to take an immediate trump trick. For example:

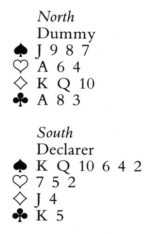

North
Dummy
♠ J 9 8 7
♡ A 6 4
♢ K Q 10
♣ A 8 3

South
Declarer
♠ K Q 10 6 4 2
♡ 7 5 2
♢ J 4
♣ K 5

West leads the jack of clubs against South's contract of four spades. An assessment of declarer's probable tricks reveals that four spades is likely to make: after knocking out the ace of spades and ace of diamonds, South has five spade tricks, one heart, two diamonds and two clubs. However, a glance at South's potential losers reveals that the situation is not so comfortable, for there is a distinct danger that the defenders might make two heart tricks as well as their two aces.

Let us suppose, for the sake of argument, that declarer wins the first club trick in the closed hand and makes the natural play of leading a trump. If the defenders win the ace and switch to hearts, their four tricks will become established, and South will have to hope that the player who has the ace of diamonds also has no more than a doubleton heart.

The best line of play is to win the club lead and play a diamond at trick two, driving out the ace. If the defenders win the diamond and switch to hearts, South can discard one of his losing hearts on the established diamond before embarking on the trump suit, and this will give him good chances of restricting himself to three losers.

IF HE HAS TO USE THE TRUMP SUIT FOR ENTRIES

Since the declaring side will usually select their best suit as trumps, it is quite likely that a fairly high proportion of their total honour strength will be situated in the trump suit. If this is the case, it may well be that the declarer will have to utilise those honour cards as the line of communication between his two hands. Here is an exaggerated example of the principle involved.

North
Dummy
♠ 7 6 5
♡ A K Q
♢ 7 4
♣ K 8 6 4 2

South
Declarer
♠ A K 3
♡ 8 7 6 4 2
♢ A 9 8 3
♣ Q

South is the declarer in four hearts. West leads the jack of clubs and, after considerable thought, East goes in with the ace and switches to a small spade.

If South wins the spade switch and draws trumps, there is no way in which he will be able to come to more than nine tricks: five hearts, two spades, one diamond and one club. In fact, the only hope of a tenth trick lies in establishing dummy's fifth club, and South has to rely on a 4–3 club break plus a 3–2 heart break. After winning the spade switch at trick two, declarer crosses to dummy with a trump and ruffs a small club; another trump to dummy is followed by a second club ruff and, providing that both opponents follow to the second round of trumps and the third round of clubs, declarer is home. He crosses to dummy with his last heart, cashes the king and 8 of clubs for his seventh and eighth tricks, and still has two aces in the closed hand to come.

IF HE HAS TO ESTABLISH ONE OR TWO RUFFS IN DUMMY

One of the principal advantages of playing in a suit contract is that it is often possible to develop an extra trick by ruffing a loser in the hand with the shorter trump holding.

North
Dummy
♡ 9 6 4

South
Declarer
♡ A K Q 7 2

Whereas this suit can never provide more than five tricks in no trumps, it will produce at least one extra trick in a heart contract if it is possible to take a ruff or two in the North hand. If the declarer is thinking along these lines, of course, he must not draw trumps before he has set up and taken the required ruffs in dummy.

A spectacular example of this kind of play occurred during the 1981 European Championships in Birmingham. The following deal comes from the match between Great Britain and Hungary.

Dealer South; love all.

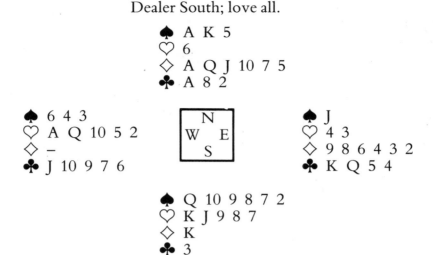

```
                  ♠ A K 5
                  ♡ 6
                  ◇ A Q J 10 7 5
                  ♣ A 8 2

   ♠ 6 4 3              N              ♠ J
   ♡ A Q 10 5 2    W         E        ♡ 4 3
   ◇ —                   S            ◇ 9 8 6 4 3 2
   ♣ J 10 9 7 6                       ♣ K Q 5 4

                  ♠ Q 10 9 8 7 2
                  ♡ K J 9 8 7
                  ◇ K
                  ♣ 3
```

The contract at both tables was six spades by South, and West led the jack of clubs to dummy's ace. The ace of spades was cashed, and East followed with the jack.

Having reached this point, an average player would probably draw trumps in three rounds and overtake the king of diamonds in dummy, banking on a 4–2 or 3–3 diamond break. A better performer might worry a little about a 5–1 diamond break, and he might play the ace and queen of spades before cashing the king of diamonds, intending to re-enter dummy with the king of spades and enjoy the rest of the diamonds. This was the line adopted by the Hungarian South player in the match, and he was extremely unlucky to be defeated when West ruffed the king of diamonds and cashed the ace of hearts.

Britain's John Collings showed how to overcome a 6–0 diamond break. He simply won the opening lead with the ace of clubs, cashed the ace of spades and led a *heart* to the third trick. He then ruffed the club return, ruffed a heart high in dummy and drew trumps. The king of diamonds was overtaken in dummy in order to provide four diamond tricks, and declarer was home: six trumps in the closed hand, the ace of clubs, four diamonds and a heart ruff in dummy gave him 12 tricks. It also gave Great Britain 17 imp in a match which they won by only 14 imp.

IF HE NEEDS TO MAKE RUFFING TRICKS IN THE HAND CONTAINING THE LONGER HOLDING IN TRUMPS

We saw above how the declarer can often increase his tally of tricks by making a ruff or two with the shorter trump holding. There are a number of less common situations in which the declarer's best line of play is to attempt to make ruffing tricks with the longer holding in trumps. These normally arise when the declarer's trumps are long but weak, and particularly when there are indications that the adverse trumps may be breaking badly. Once again, of course, the declarer must not attempt to draw trumps first. Here is an interesting example of this type of play from the match between Taiwan and Norway in the 1980 World Bridge Olympiad.

Dealer East; North–South vulnerable.

```
                    ♠ A 10 8 7
                    ♡ A K
                    ♢ A K 10 5
                    ♣ 10 8 4

      ♠ K Q J 3        ┌─────────┐        ♠ 9 5 4 2
      ♡ 4 3            │    N    │        ♡ Q J 5 2
      ♢ Q 8 3          │ W     E │        ♢ J 9 6
      ♣ A K J 2        │    S    │        ♣ Q 3
                       └─────────┘
                    ♠ 6
                    ♡ 10 9 8 7 6
                    ♢ 7 4 2
                    ♣ 9 7 6 5
```

When Norway held the North–South cards, the bidding was as follows:

South	West	North	East
			NB
NB	1♣(1)	NB	1♢(2)
NB	1NT	Dble(3)	NB
2♡	NB	NB	Dble(4)
NB	NB	NB	

(1) A strong opening bid, showing 16 or more points and any distribution.

(2) Showing 0–7 points.

(3) I fully agree with North's bidding on this board. While I am certain that it pays to intervene immediately on weak hands over artificial one club bids, I am equally certain that the best policy on strong hands is to pass on the first round and enter the auction at a later stage, after you have had a chance to assess where the balance of the points is likely to be.

(4) This was an aggressive double, but East knew that his side had at least six trumps and at least 22 high-card points.

West led the king of spades against two hearts doubled, and South won in dummy and immediately ruffed a spade. A diamond to the king, a spade ruff, the ace of diamonds and another spade ruff gave declarer six tricks, and dummy's ace and king of trumps were still intact to provide two more. Plus 670 to Norway in what turned out to be a crucial match.

IF HE PLANS TO EXECUTE A DUMMY REVERSAL PLAY

Taking the last example one stage further, we find another play which involves not drawing trumps until later in the proceedings: the dummy reversal.

North
Dummy
♡ Q J 10

South
Declarer
♡ A K 7 4 2

The above heart suit can never produce more than five tricks in no trumps. If South is the declarer in a heart contract, however, there are two ways in which he might be able to wangle an extra trick. One possibility is to make a ruffing trick in dummy – the type of play which we noted earlier, when the declarer has to establish one or two ruffs in a dummy. Alternatively, it may be possible to ruff three times with the longer trump holding and then draw trumps with the Q–J–10. This is known as a dummy reversal, presumably because one makes dummy the master hand and contradicts normal card-play principles by seeking ruffs in the hand containing the longer trump holding. An interesting example of this type of play occurred during the 16th International Bridge Festival in Israel.

Dealer South; East–West vulnerable.

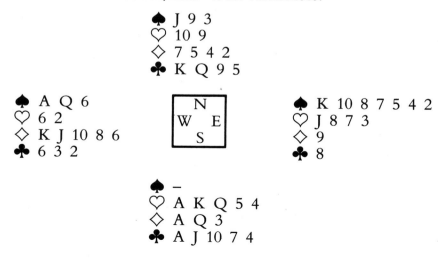

♠ J 9 3
♡ 10 9
♢ 7 5 4 2
♣ K Q 9 5

♠ A Q 6
♡ 6 2
♢ K J 10 8 6
♣ 6 3 2

♠ K 10 8 7 5 4 2
♡ J 8 7 3
♢ 9
♣ 8

♠ –
♡ A K Q 5 4
♢ A Q 3
♣ A J 10 7 4

When the hand first occurred in the Swiss Teams Event, I was not too pleased about my performance.

South	West	North	East
	Ellenberg		Mrs Markus
1♣(1)	NB	1♢(2)	3♠
4♡	4♠	Dble	NB
NB	NB		

(1) Our opponents were playing the Precision Club system, and one club showed any hand containing 16 or more points.
(2) A negative response, showing 0–7 points.

I was a little unlucky to lose 500 in four spades doubled and, since our team-mates lost 50 in the sound contract of six clubs, this was an expensive board for my team. It was not until the next day that we realised that six clubs should probably have been made. South ruffs the ace of spades lead, crosses to dummy with a club and ruffs another spade with the jack. Another club to dummy and a spade ruff with the ace of trumps leaves the following position:

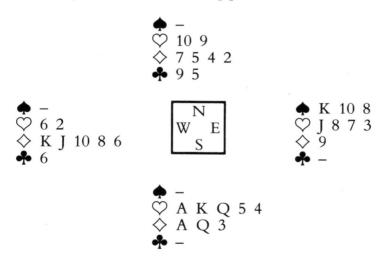

South now plays the ace and king of hearts and ruffs a heart in dummy. The 9 of clubs draws the outstanding trump, South discarding one of his losing diamonds, and declarer makes three of the last four tricks by way of two hearts and the ace of diamonds. Seven club tricks, four hearts and the ace of diamonds would have given North–South +920 instead of −50, and it would have been most satisfying to make a slam by means of a perfect dummy reversal.

An essential ingredient of the dummy reversal is a good trump holding in dummy, so that declarer can eventually draw the opponents' trumps with the shorter holding. Moreover, the fact that dummy has a good three- or four-card trump holding often means that declarer cannot make the more normal play of ruffing losers in dummy, for to do so may establish a trump trick for the defence. This is another factor which may persuade declarer to prefer to execute a dummy reversal. Here is a good example from rubber bridge, when George Lengyel contrived to bid and make a small slam with a combined point-count of 19.

Dealer South; love all.

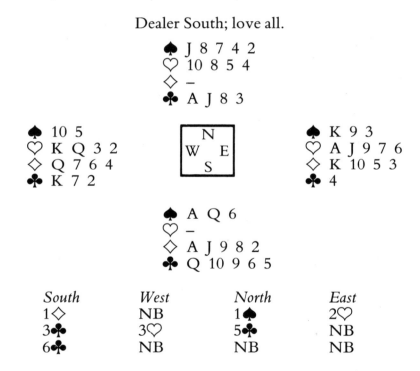

♠ J 8 7 4 2
♥ 10 8 5 4
♦ —
♣ A J 8 3

♠ 10 5   ♠ K 9 3
♥ K Q 3 2   ♥ A J 9 7 6
♦ Q 7 6 4   ♦ K 10 5 3
♣ K 7 2   ♣ 4

♠ A Q 6
♥ —
♦ A J 9 8 2
♣ Q 10 9 6 5

South	West	North	East
1♦	NB	1♠	2♥
3♣	3♥	5♣	NB
6♣	NB	NB	NB

West led the king of hearts, and South ruffed high and led a small club to dummy's 8, which held the trick. Another heart was ruffed high and a small club to the jack allowed Lengyel to ruff a third heart. He then cashed the ace of diamonds, discarding dummy's last heart, and exited with the queen of spades to East's king. The 3–2 spade break meant that there were no further problems on the hand, and declarer was eventually able to ruff a diamond in dummy, draw the one outstanding trump, and cash the established spade tricks for 12 tricks in all.

My next example also occurred at the rubber bridge table. In many ways, it is typical of the kind of bridge which is played in the high-stake games at the London Clubs – the hands are exciting, the bidding is a little crude, and the card-play is of an extremely high standard. The declarer was once again George Lengyel, who seems to specialise in this kind of play.

Dealer South; love all.

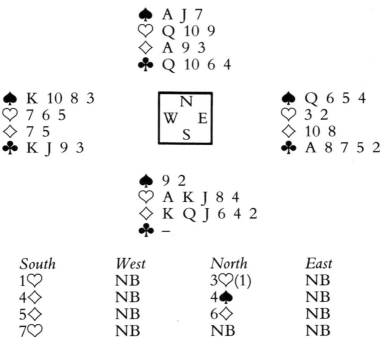

♠ A J 7
♡ Q 10 9
◇ A 9 3
♣ Q 10 6 4

♠ K 10 8 3
♡ 7 6 5
◇ 7 5
♣ K J 9 3

♠ Q 6 5 4
♡ 3 2
◇ 10 8
♣ A 8 7 5 2

♠ 9 2
♡ A K J 8 4
◇ K Q J 6 4 2
♣ —

South	West	North	East
1♡	NB	3♡(1)	NB
4◇	NB	4♠	NB
5◇	NB	6◇	NB
7♡	NB	NB	NB

(1) A jump raise is often played as forcing in rubber bridge circles.

As all the best bridge books recommend, West led a trump against the grand slam. It looks at first sight as if declarer has an unavoidable spade loser, but Lengyel found a neat solution. He won the trump lead in dummy, ruffed a club high and crossed to dummy with another trump. A second club ruff was followed by a spade to the ace and a third club ruff. Declarer now crossed to dummy with the ace of diamonds, cashed the queen of hearts to draw West's last trump and to provide a resting-place for his spade loser, and made the rest of the tricks with diamonds. South's 13 tricks were one spade, six diamonds and, thanks to the dummy reversal, three trumps in dummy and three club ruffs in the closed hand.

The dummy reversal just described produced the vital 13th trick in a grand slam. On my final example, a similar play succeeded only in landing an overtrick in a match-pointed pairs contest, but it serves to illustrate the point that opportunities for dummy reversals are more frequent in actual play than might be imagined. This deal occurred during the 1981 Guardian Easter Tournament, when I was partnered by the German international, Dirk Schroeder.

Dealer South; love all.

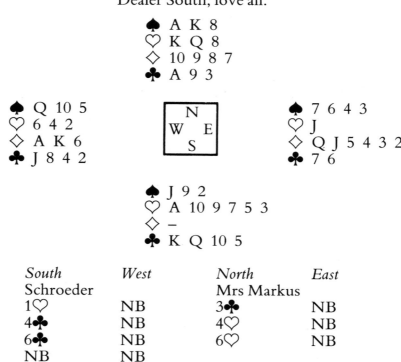

```
                    ♠ A K 8
                    ♡ K Q 8
                    ◇ 10 9 8 7
                    ♣ A 9 3
  ♠ Q 10 5                              ♠ 7 6 4 3
  ♡ 6 4 2            N                  ♡ J
  ◇ A K 6        W       E              ◇ Q J 5 4 3 2
  ♣ J 8 4 2          S                  ♣ 7 6
                    ♠ J 9 2
                    ♡ A 10 9 7 5 3
                    ◇ –
                    ♣ K Q 10 5
```

South	West	North	East
Schroeder		Mrs Markus	
1♡	NB	3♣	NB
4♣	NB	4♡	NB
6♣	NB	6♡	NB
NB	NB		

West led the ace of diamonds against six hearts, and Dirk Schroeder was quick to see that a dummy reversal play would make certain of his contract and give him fair chances of an overtrick. He ruffed the diamond and used dummy's spade entries to ruff two more diamonds. A heart to the king dropped the jack from East, and declarer then ruffed dummy's last diamond with the ace of hearts, leaving the following position:

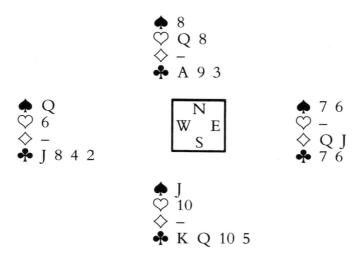

```
                     ♠ 8
                     ♡ Q 8
                     ◇ —
                     ♣ A 9 3

  ♠ Q                ┌─────────┐              ♠ 7 6
  ♡ 6                │    N    │              ♡ —
  ◇ —                │ W     E │              ◇ Q J
  ♣ J 8 4 2          │    S    │              ♣ 7 6
                     └─────────┘
                     ♠ J
                     ♡ 10
                     ◇ —
                     ♣ K Q 10 5
```

West had already been forced to under-ruff on the fourth round of diamonds, and he was fatally squeezed when declarer cashed the last two trumps in dummy. Since he had to retain the queen of spades in order to guard dummy's 8, he was forced to let a club go and South's fourth club became established.

IF HE PLANS TO PLAY ALONG CROSS RUFF LINES

Let us have another look at the 5–3 heart fit which we considered in connection with the theory of the dummy reversal play.

North
Dummy
♡ Q J 10

South
Declarer
♡ A K 7 4 2

We saw earlier how the declarer would winkle an extra trick out of the trump suit if he were able to make three ruffs in the South hand and subsequently draw trumps with dummy's strong three-card holding. However, six tricks is not the maximum number which declarer can make from this suit: if he can arrange to make three ruffs in dummy and three low ruffs in the closed hand, he will make eight heart tricks in all. This is the principle of the cross ruff.

A cross ruff proved to be the only successful line of play on the following famous hand from the US Winter Nationals of 1947, when the late Harry Fishbein was the only player to bid and make game.

Dealer South; North–South vulnerable.

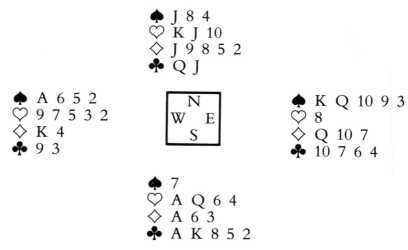

♠ J 8 4
♡ K J 10
♢ J 9 8 5 2
♣ Q J

♠ A 6 5 2   ♠ K Q 10 9 3
♡ 9 7 5 3 2   ♡ 8
♢ K 4   ♢ Q 10 7
♣ 9 3   ♣ 10 7 6 4

♠ 7
♡ A Q 6 4
♢ A 6 3
♣ A K 8 5 2

The bidding:

South	West	North	East
1♣	NB	1♦	1♠
2♡	2♠	3♡	NB
4♡	NB	NB	NB

When John Griffiths recalls this hand in his interesting collection of famous deals entitled *The Golden Years of Bridge*, he writes as follows:

'West led the ace of spades and then a low spade.

'Some Souths tried to make an overtrick, hoping for a 3–3 break in trumps. They ruffed in hand, entered dummy with a club, ruffed a second spade and led the ace of trumps and then a trump to dummy's king. Two down gave them a deservedly bottom score.

'Most declarers were content to play for their contract, discarding diamonds on the second and third rounds of spades. This play would have succeeded if both hearts and clubs had broken no worse than 4–2, but failed against the 5–1 trump break. However, they went down only one.

'Fishbein saw that dummy's high trumps were ideal for a cross ruff. He therefore trumped the second spade, led a low club to dummy and returned a club to his ace. Note that the 'natural' spade return to be ruffed in hand would have left him an entry short to give dummy three club ruffs.

'Declarer next led the king of clubs to give dummy its first ruff, but as the cards lay West was forced to trump first. Dummy's last spade was then ruffed low, a second club was ruffed in dummy and the ace of diamonds provided the entry for South to ruff his fifth club. The ace and queen of trumps were still in South's hand to make his ten tricks.

'This display of virtuosity rightly earned Fishbein a top, though students of the game will notice that if West had followed Dr Stern's dictum of always leading trumps with five, Fishbein could not have made his contract. Indeed, he would go two down unless he played for the 5–1 split and did not try to fulfil his contract by drawing trumps.'

In a perfect cross ruff, the declarer cashes all his side-suit winners, in case the defenders are able to discard their losers in those suits while the cross ruff is in operation, and then cross ruffs with high trumps in both hands. However, there are a number of variations on this theme. For example, it is often best to cross ruff high first and low later, in case a defender is able to over-ruff and return a trump:

North
Dummy
♠ A Q 10 7

South
Declarer
♠ K J 9 6

If declarer needs seven spade tricks from this holding, he might do best to cross ruff with the six top trumps first and then develop the seventh trick by ruffing another loser with either the 6 or 7 of spades.

Similarly, there are a large number of deals on which a partial cross ruff is the winning line of play. Here is an interesting example from the third International Romanian ACR Bridge Festival.

Dealer West; East–West vulnerable.

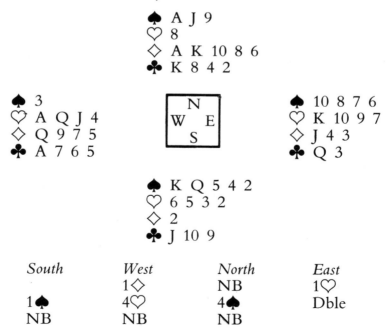

```
                  ♠ A J 9
                  ♡ 8
                  ♢ A K 10 8 6
                  ♣ K 8 4 2

  ♠ 3                              ♠ 10 8 7 6
  ♡ A Q J 4        N               ♡ K 10 9 7
  ♢ Q 9 7 5      W   E             ♢ J 4 3
  ♣ A 7 6 5        S               ♣ Q 3

                  ♠ K Q 5 4 2
                  ♡ 6 5 3 2
                  ♢ 2
                  ♣ J 10 9
```

South	West	North	East
	1◇	NB	1♡
1♠	4♡	4♠	Dble
NB	NB	NB	

West led the ace and another heart against four spades doubled. Declarer ruffed in dummy, cashed two top diamonds throwing a club, and ruffed a diamond in the closed hand. He then led the jack of clubs, and West went up with the ace and switched to a trump. South won with dummy's ace, cashed the king of clubs and led another diamond from dummy. East had to ruff in order to force out a high trump from declarer, and this left the following position:

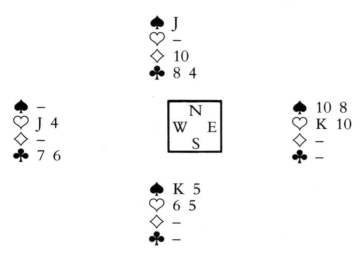

South ruffed a heart for his eighth trick and led the established eight of clubs from dummy. East had to ruff, whereupon declarer discarded his losing heart and made the last two tricks with the king and 5 of spades.

IF HE NEEDS TO GUARD AGAINST A BAD TRUMP BREAK

The declarer's play of the last contract was obviously guided by the opposition bidding and by East's double of the final call. In fact, another common reason for not drawing trumps is that the bidding has indicated that there will be a bad break in the suit. Here is that man George Lengyel in action again at the rubber bridge table.

Dealer South; love all.

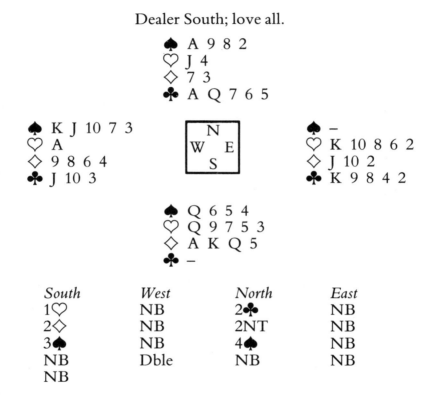

```
                ♠ A 9 8 2
                ♡ J 4
                ◇ 7 3
                ♣ A Q 7 6 5

♠ K J 10 7 3        N          ♠ —
♡ A            W       E       ♡ K 10 8 6 2
◇ 9 8 6 4           S          ◇ J 10 2
♣ J 10 3                       ♣ K 9 8 4 2

                ♠ Q 6 5 4
                ♡ Q 9 7 5 3
                ◇ A K Q 5
                ♣ —
```

South	West	North	East
1♡	NB	2♣	NB
2◇	NB	2NT	NB
3♠	NB	4♠	NB
NB	Dble	NB	NB
NB			

Doubles of this kind can give a lot away. On this occasion, Lengyel decided to assume that West had doubled on the strength of a powerful holding in trumps, and he planned the play accordingly.

West cashed the ace of hearts and then made the fatal error of switching to the jack of clubs. The ace of clubs and a club ruff were followed by three top diamonds, with South discarding a heart from dummy. A diamond ruff and a second club ruff left the following ending:

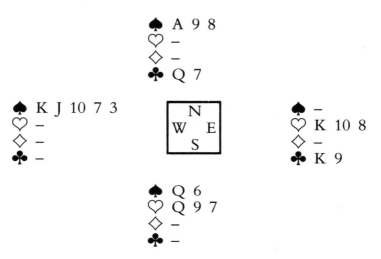

A heart from the closed hand now put West into a hopeless position. No matter what he did, he could not come to more than two trump tricks: if he ruffed low, dummy would over-ruff and exit with a club; and if West ruffed the heart high, dummy would discard a club and eventually come to a second trump trick by force.

On occasions, of course, it can be correct to attempt to cater for a bad trump break even if you have less reason to suspect that there might be one. An interesting deal with this theme occurred during the Gold Cup semi–finals in 1981.

Dealer North; love all.

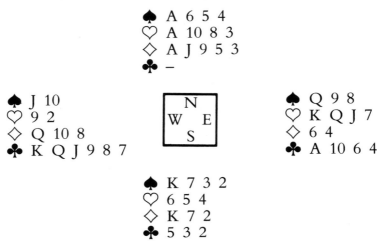

♠ A 6 5 4
♡ A 10 8 3
◇ A J 9 5 3
♣ –

♠ J 10   ♠ Q 9 8
♡ 9 2   ♡ K Q J 7
◇ Q 10 8   ◇ 6 4
♣ K Q J 9 8 7   ♣ A 10 6 4

♠ K 7 3 2
♡ 6 5 4
◇ K 7 2
♣ 5 3 2

At one table in the match, South became the declarer in four spades after East had made a take-out double of North's opening bid of one diamond. West led the king of clubs, and declarer ruffed in dummy and cashed the ace of spades, on which West dropped the jack. South now played a diamond to the king and finessed the jack of diamonds. Convinced by the bidding and play that East held four trumps, he continued with the ace of diamonds. East ruffed and switched to the king of hearts, and declarer won in dummy and played another winning diamond, ruffed by East with the queen of spades. South could not afford to over-ruff, and he therefore discarded a heart loser. However, East fired back the queen and jack of hearts, promoting a trump trick for West and defeating the contract by one trick.

The same contract was reached at the other table, but East–West had only competed in clubs and there was less reason for South to fear a 4–1 spade break. He ruffed the opening club lead, cashed the king of diamonds and successfully finessed dummy's jack. He then cashed two top spades and claimed 11 tricks when both opponents followed twice.

In my view, South was quite right to worry about a bad spade break. He did well not to draw trumps too early, but his timing at the first table was not quite correct. The best play is to ruff the club lead, cash the king of diamonds and play a diamond to the jack. When this holds, continue with the ace of diamonds immediately. If East does not ruff, you can cash the ace and king of trumps, ruff a club and continue with diamonds, thereby making ten tricks even if the trumps are 4–1. East must therefore ruff the third diamond, but this leaves South in complete control even if East started life with four trumps.

IF HE PLANS TO END-PLAY ONE OF THE OPPONENTS IN TRUMPS

We saw earlier the way in which a penalty double can sometimes alert the declarer to the danger of a bad trump break and enable him to find an unusual line of play in order to make his contract. There is another way in which the opponents' bidding can help the declarer in the play of a suit contract: if the majority of the high-card strength seems likely to be concentrated in one defender's hand, it may be best to eschew the more normal finesses and attempt to end-play the defender in question in the trump suit. This will once again involve not tackling trumps too early, and the declarer found a clever example of this type of play on the following deal from the 1981 'Varsity match between Oxford and Cambridge.

Dealer South; North–South vulnerable.

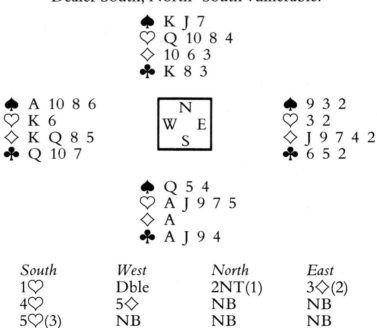

```
                ♠ K J 7
                ♡ Q 10 8 4
                ♢ 10 6 3
                ♣ K 8 3

♠ A 10 8 6          N           ♠ 9 3 2
♡ K 6          W         E      ♡ 3 2
♢ K Q 8 5           S           ♢ J 9 7 4 2
♣ Q 10 7                        ♣ 6 5 2

                ♠ Q 5 4
                ♡ A J 9 7 5
                ♢ A
                ♣ A J 9 4
```

South	West	North	East
1♡	Dble	2NT(1)	3♢(2)
4♡	5♢	NB	NB
5♡(3)	NB	NB	NB

(1) Since 2NT is not required in a natural sense after an intervening double, it is normally used to show a sound raise to at least three of the opener's suit. North was certainly not holding back when he bid 2NT on this particular nine-loser hand.

(2) And neither was East.

(3) Five diamonds doubled would actually have been quite profitable, but the vulnerability persuaded South to push on to five hearts.

West led the king of diamonds to declarer's ace. Since West's bidding made it quite likely that the king of hearts and queen of clubs were both lying unfavourably, South decided to attempt an elimination play. He therefore postponed drawing trumps, and led the queen of spades at trick two. West won with the ace and tried to cash the queen of diamonds, but declarer ruffed, cashed the ace of hearts and two top spades and ruffed another diamond in the closed hand. He then exited with a heart, and West was end-played. He had to choose between leading a club into South's tenace and conceding a ruff and discard in spades or diamonds; in either case South was bound to take the rest of the tricks and land his precarious contract.

My next example occurred during the Northern Ireland regional final of the Sobranie Challenge Cup, an inter-club team of four event.

Dealer South; North–South vulnerable.

```
              ♠ Q 10 7
              ♡ 10 9 8 7 4
              ◇ K Q
              ♣ Q J 7

♠ A 8 2            N            ♠ J 6 5 4
♡ K Q 3       W       E         ♡ 2
◇ J 10 9 7         S            ◇ 8 5 4 3
♣ 6 5 3                         ♣ K 10 9 2

              ♠ K 9 3
              ♡ A J 6 5
              ◇ A 6 2
              ♣ A 8 4
```

South	West	North	East
1♡	NB	3♡	NB
4♡	NB	NB	NB

South won the opening diamond lead in dummy and, concentrating solely on making the recommended book play in the trump suit, he ran the 10 of hearts at trick two. West won with the queen and continued with a second diamond to dummy's king. Another heart from dummy revealed the bad news, and declarer went up with the ace, cashed the ace of diamonds to dispose of dummy's small club, and exited with a trump. West won with the king and defended well by switching to a club, leaving South to locate the jack of spades for his contract. Justice was done when declarer guessed wrongly by finessing the 10 of spades in dummy, going one down in a contract which he really should have made.

Study the effect of winning the diamond lead in dummy and, before tackling the trumps, running the queen of clubs at the second trick. When this holds, South cashes the king of diamonds, crosses to hand with the ace of hearts and discards a club on the ace of diamonds. He then cashes the ace of clubs and ruffs a club in dummy before exiting with a trump. The defenders can take two heart tricks but, no matter who wins the last heart, he will be compelled to open up the spade suit to the declarer's advantage.

IF HE PLANS TO DISCOVER MORE ABOUT THE UNSEEN HANDS BEFORE DECIDING HOW TO PLAY THE TRUMP SUIT

If there is more than one way of handling the trump suit, the declarer should delay taking his decision for as long as possible, so that he gives himself every chance of picking up all the available clues. Consider this interesting deal from a special pairs tournament which was organised to herald the opening of the new Leicester Bridge Centre.

Dealer East; North–South vulnerable.

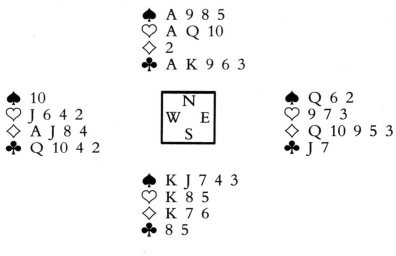

```
                    ♠ A 9 8 5
                    ♡ A Q 10
                    ♢ 2
                    ♣ A K 9 6 3

♠ 10                                        ♠ Q 6 2
♡ J 6 4 2           N                       ♡ 9 7 3
♢ A J 8 4        W     E                    ♢ Q 10 9 5 3
♣ Q 10 4 2          S                       ♣ J 7

                    ♠ K J 7 4 3
                    ♡ K 8 5
                    ♢ K 7 6
                    ♣ 8 5
```

South Brock	West	North Mrs Markus	East
			NB
NB	NB	1♣	NB
1♠	NB	3♡	NB
3NT	NB	4♠	NB
4NT	NB	5♠	NB
6♠	NB	NB	NB

Raymond Brock and I did well to reach the excellent contract of six spades on the North–South cards, but my partner soon went one down when he won the opening heart lead and played the ace and king of spades.

'You know that spades never break', I teased, referring to a popular rubber bridge superstition. 'You should have finessed the jack when East followed to the second round.'

'You are quite right', Raymond replied, 'but for completely the wrong reason. I should have tested the diamond suit by playing a small diamond to the king at trick two. When West produced the ace of diamonds, I should have finessed the jack of spades on the second round of trumps, for most defenders would cash a side-suit ace at trick one if they held a possible trump trick in their hand'.

Raymond was quite right, of course, and this is an excellent example of the way a good player should approach a problem. It is surprising how often you can find a pointer to the correct solution when you are faced with what at first sight appears to be a complete guess.

IF HE NEEDS TO ESTABLISH A SIDE SUIT FIRST

Although I have listed this as the tenth possible reason for not drawing trumps at the earliest opportunity, it is actually one of the most important: it is very often correct to set to work on the establishment of an important side suit first.

Sometimes, the decision to play on a side suit first may be thrust upon the declarer by the threat of a forcing defence. Rob Sheehan did very well, for example, to retain control of this tricky hand from a Bermuda Bowl match between Great Britain and Poland.

Dealer South; game all.

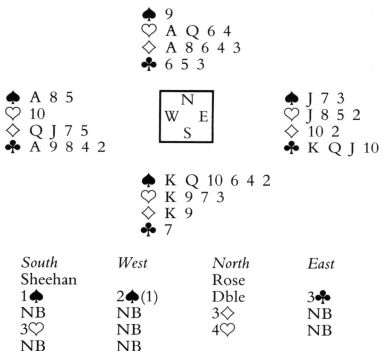

South	West	North	East
Sheehan		Rose	
1♠	2♠(1)	Dble	3♣
NB	NB	3◇	NB
3♡	NB	4♡	NB
NB	NB		

(1) Showing both minor suits.

West led the ace and another club against four hearts, and Sheehan ruffed the second round and crossed to dummy with a trump to lead the 9 of spades to the 3, 10 and ace. West returned another club, and declarer ruffed and cashed the king of hearts, discovering the not unexpected 4–1 break. He then turned his attention to the spade suit, cashing the king and queen to discard the diamond losers from dummy. East was able to ruff the fourth spade, but that was the last trick for the defence: South ruffed the club return in dummy, drew the outstanding trump and cashed two diamond winners to make his vulnerable game. Unfortunately, the British pair at the other table elected to sacrifice in five clubs, and we shall therefore never know whether the Polish declarer would have found the same inspired solution to the problem of how to make four hearts.

Sometimes, of course, the case for establishing a side suit first may simply be that it is safer to use high trumps as communications between the two hands than to rely on favourable breaks at a later stage. For example, South played with great care and accuracy on the following deal from rubber bridge.

Dealer South; game all.

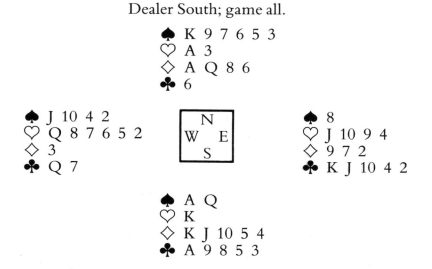

South found himself in the perfect contract of seven diamonds against the opening lead of the 2 of hearts. Having carefully considered all the possible pitfalls, South came up with a neat way of making sure of his important contract. He won the heart lead in the closed hand, cashed the ace of spades and crossed to dummy with a trump in order to discard his remaining spade on the ace of hearts. A spade ruff, another diamond to dummy and a second spade ruff established dummy's long suit. The king of diamonds now drew East's last trump, and the ace of clubs and a club ruff provided access to the established spades. Four spades, two hearts, six diamonds and one club trick gave South his grand slam with the minimum risk.

Finally, we come to a category of play which I always call 'playing with a second trump suit'. This involves establishing a long side suit and subsequently using it to regain control of the hand which would otherwise be lost for ever. Here is a typical example from the 1981 Guardian Easter Tournament.

Dealer East; game all.

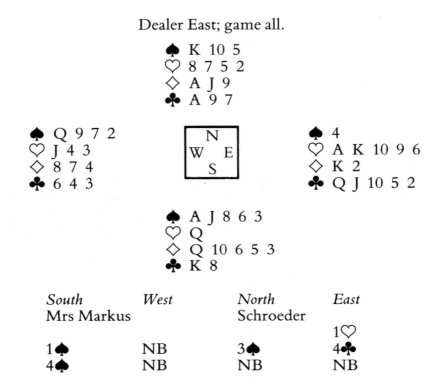

South	West	North	East
Mrs Markus		Schroeder	
			1♡
1♠	NB	3♠	4♣
4♠	NB	NB	NB

The defence began with two top hearts, and I ruffed the second round and immediately played a diamond to the jack and king, establishing my second suit. East continued with a third heart, and I ruffed with the jack of spades. West now had more trumps than I did, but East's bidding made it fairly easy to assess the position. I cashed the ace of spades, played a spade to dummy's 10 and cashed the king of spades, leaving one trump at large in the West hand. I then began to cash my established diamonds, and West was powerless. He eventually ruffed and switched to a club, but the king of clubs provided access to my remaining diamonds and I had restricted my losers to one heart, one diamond and one spade.

This kind of hand always looks impressive in print. However, the winning play was not too difficult to find once I had brought into operation two of my basic principles of declarer's play: first, listen to the bidding and remember it during the play; and second, don't play trumps too early – there may be more important things to do first.

A similar play was found by Martin Hoffman when I played with him in a tournament in Le Touquet. Martin is one of the most brilliant match-pointed pairs specialists in the country, and he is also one of the fastest players and analysts of all time. Here is a typical example of his great skill.

Dealer West; North–South vulnerable.

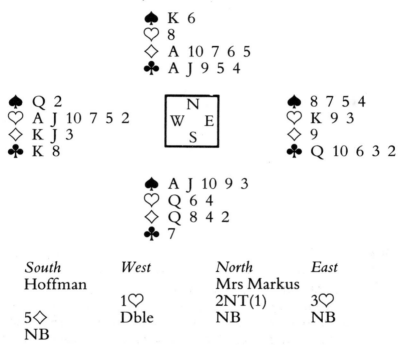

```
              ♠ K 6
              ♡ 8
              ♢ A 10 7 6 5
              ♣ A J 9 5 4

♠ Q 2                    N              ♠ 8 7 5 4
♡ A J 10 7 5 2      W         E         ♡ K 9 3
♢ K J 3                  S              ♢ 9
♣ K 8                                   ♣ Q 10 6 3 2

              ♠ A J 10 9 3
              ♡ Q 6 4
              ♢ Q 8 4 2
              ♣ 7
```

South	West	North	East
Hoffman		Mrs Markus	
	1♡	2NT(1)	3♡
5♢	Dble	NB	NB
NB			

(1) The so-called 'unusual' 2NT overcall, showing at least 5–5 in the minor suits.

West led the ace and another heart, ruffed in dummy. Hoffman played a small diamond to the queen and king, and West persevered with a third round of hearts. Declarer ruffed in dummy, cashed the ace of clubs and ruffed a club in the closed hand. He then led the jack of spades to the queen and king, and returned to hand with the ace of spades, leaving the following position:

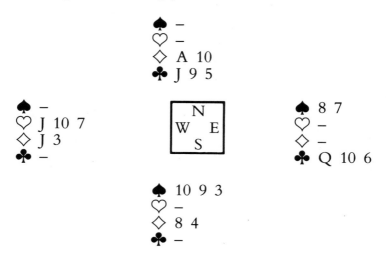

Hoffman could not take the marked trump finesse without locking himself in dummy, but he found a neat solution to his problem: he started to cash his winning spades – his 'second trump suit'. West was in an impossible position. If he ruffed a spade, declarer could over-ruff in dummy, cash the ace of diamonds and ruff a club back to hand to cash the remaining spade tricks; and if West declined to ruff, declarer could discard three club losers from dummy and take the trump finesse at the 12th trick.

Finally, a hand from television's *Master Bridge* series on which Irving Rose could not make the mistake of drawing trumps too early – for the simple reason that one of the opponents had more trumps than he did. However, the existence of a 'second trump suit' enabled Rose to land his grand slam.

Dealer East; East–West vulnerable.

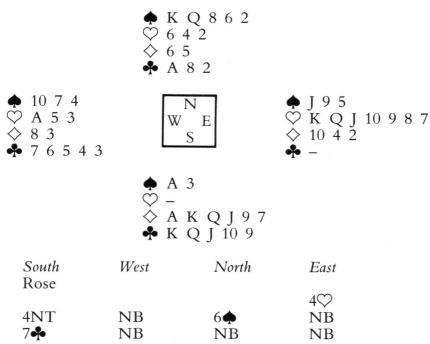

```
              ♠ K Q 8 6 2
              ♡ 6 4 2
              ◇ 6 5
              ♣ A 8 2

♠ 10 7 4          ┌───────┐          ♠ J 9 5
♡ A 5 3           │   N   │          ♡ K Q J 10 9 8 7
◇ 8 3             │ W   E │          ◇ 10 4 2
♣ 7 6 5 4 3       │   S   │          ♣ –
                  └───────┘
              ♠ A 3
              ♡ –
              ◇ A K Q J 9 7
              ♣ K Q J 10 9
```

South	West	North	East
Rose			
			4♡
4NT	NB	6♠	NB
7♣	NB	NB	NB

Irving Rose made the play look easy. He ruffed the opening heart lead and played the jack of clubs to discover the bad news. He then played a spade to dummy's queen, the key play, and embarked on his diamond suit. West was helpless. If he ruffed a diamond, declarer would over ruff in dummy and draw the outstanding trumps; and if West declined to ruff a diamond, South would discard the remaining four spades from dummy and cross ruff the remainder of the tricks.

This hand seems quite straightforward when one reads about it after the event. At the table, however, only players of Irving Rose's calibre are likely to find the winning line of play, and this ability to find tricky plays under pressure separates the real top experts from the average-to-good players.

DEFENCE

8   A Leading Question

Most standard text-books on the game set out tables showing which card you should lead from various suit combinations. I do not propose to do the same in these pages, because I do not have particularly strong views on the subject: I would just like to say that I have been employing what are normally called 'standard' leads for more years than I care to remember, and that I still see no compelling reason to change my methods.

In my view, the problem facing the opening leader is normally not which card to lead from a particular suit: it is which suit to lead from a particular hand, and this is a topic which is not always well covered in text-books. The important question to ask yourself when you are contemplating your opening lead is whether you should be looking for an attacking lead or a passive one. My philosophy is that you should attack whenever possible. I have never heard of any generals who have won battles by adopting purely cautious tactics and, unless you take some risks, too many contracts will make which should be defeated. It is perfectly true, of course, that too much courage and daring in connection with your initial salvo will occasionally misfire, but I am absolutely certain that positive thinking pays when you are weighing up your opening lead.

ATTACKING LEADS

I am often asked for advice on the difficult subject of opening leads, and it might be helpful if I set out below one or two ideas on the sort of situations in which you should be looking for an attacking opening lead.

(*a*) An attacking lead often takes the form of a lead of a suit suggested by your partner during the auction. Generally speaking, if partner has indicated the point of attack by bidding or doubling, you should lead that suit. If you do this and your attack fails, you will find that your partner will be very understanding; on the other hand, he may well be completely lacking in sympathy if you ignore his suggestion and make an unsuccessful lead in another suit.

I was reminded of this first Golden Rule of leading by the following fascinating deal from Channel 4's successful television programme, *Master Bridge*.

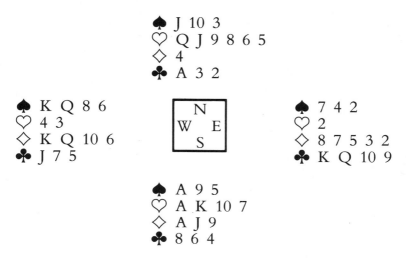

♠ J 10 3
♡ Q J 9 8 6 5
♢ 4
♣ A 3 2

♠ K Q 8 6
♡ 4 3
♢ K Q 10 6
♣ J 7 5

N
W E
S

♠ 7 4 2
♡ 2
♢ 8 7 5 3 2
♣ K Q 10 9

♠ A 9 5
♡ A K 10 7
♢ A J 9
♣ 8 6 4

When I was playing with Mrs Jane Priday, the brilliant Pakistani champion, Zia Mahmoud, reached four hearts in two bids: he opened one heart on the South hand, and his partner raised confidently to four.

That confidence was not misplaced. As there was nothing in the bidding to indicate a club lead, Jane made the natural, attacking lead of the king of diamonds. Zia promptly ducked in both hands, hoping that a diamond continuation would enable him to discard both dummy's club losers. However, my partner found an excellent switch to the 5 of clubs and, with both spade honours lying badly, Zia was still in danger of losing four tricks.

The Pakistani's superb card-play technique saw him home. He went up with dummy's ace of clubs, drew trumps in two rounds and cashed the ace of diamonds, discarding a club from dummy. He then led the jack of diamonds, throwing dummy's remaining club when West covered with the queen. Jane exited safely with a second round of clubs, but the end was nigh. Zia ruffed in dummy, crossed to hand with a trump and ruffed his last club. He then ran the jack of spades to the queen, and my unfortunate partner was end-played and forced to concede a ruff and discard or return a second spade into South's tenace.

At the other table, the auction was much longer.

South	West	North	East
1NT(1)	NB	2♢(2)	NB
3♡(3)	NB	4♣(4)	Dble(5)
4♡	NB	NB	NB

(1) Showing 15–17 points.
(2) A transfer bid, requesting the opener to bid two hearts.
(3) Showing particularly good support for hearts.
(4) A cue bid.
(5) Suggesting a club lead.

As you will see, if West had made the disciplined lead of a small club, South would have had no chance of making four hearts. In actual fact, however, West ignored his partner's helpful double and led the king of diamonds. Declarer could now have made his contract by adopting Zia Mahmoud's line of play, but he adopted the lazy, 75 per cent line of relying on one of two spade finesses and went one down.

(b) Generally speaking, you should look for an attacking lead against 3NT. The declarer will more often than not be able to accumulate nine tricks if he is given time to manoeuvre, and the play of 3NT often takes the form of a race by the defenders to develop five tricks before the declarer can develop nine. If your partner has not bid, you should normally attack by leading your longest suit, and there is a lot to be said for the late Leslie Dodds' maxim that you should always lead the fourth highest card of your longest suit unless you have a very good reason for not doing so.

Some players are extremely reluctant to lead their long suit when they have a bad hand, but my experience suggests that this reticence is overdone. Here is another interesting hand from the same *Master Bridge* series.

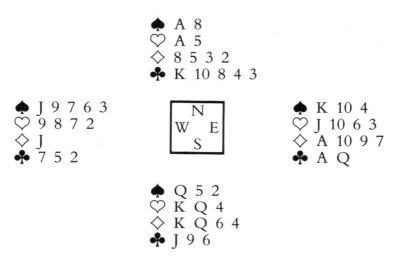

```
              ♠ A 8
              ♡ A 5
              ◇ 8 5 3 2
              ♣ K 10 8 4 3

  ♠ J 9 7 6 3      ┌─────────┐      ♠ K 10 4
  ♡ 9 8 7 2        │    N    │      ♡ J 10 6 3
  ◇ J              │  W   E  │      ◇ A 10 9 7
  ♣ 7 5 2          │    S    │      ♣ A Q
                   └─────────┘
              ♠ Q 5 2
              ♡ K Q 4
              ◇ K Q 6 4
              ♣ J 9 6
```

The final contract at both tables was 2NT. When I held the East cards, my partner selected the cautious lead of the 9 of hearts. We no longer had time to develop the spade suit, and the declarer was able to scramble eight tricks by playing on clubs.

At the other table, Irving Rose made the attacking lead of the 6 of spades and gave his partner, Martin Hoffman, a chance to execute a typically brilliant defence. Martin had to think quickly when South ducked the first spade in dummy but, as usual, he found the winning solution in no time at all: he inserted the 10 of spades to drive out declarer's queen. This enabled East to return the king on the second round of the suit, leaving himself with the 4 of spades as a means of reaching his partner's hand.

Martin Hoffman's reasoning for this brilliant defensive shot was quite simple. He knew that his partner had very few high-card points and no side-suit entry for his spades. By forcing declarer to use one of his spade guards at trick one, on the other hand, East was able to establish a definite line of communication with his partner's hand. Declarer was therefore forced to lose two club tricks, the ace of diamonds and three long spades.

A board from the 1984 'Varsity Match, which Oxford won by the narrow margin of 2 imp, illustrates the case for attacking leads against no trump contracts.

Dealer North; game all.

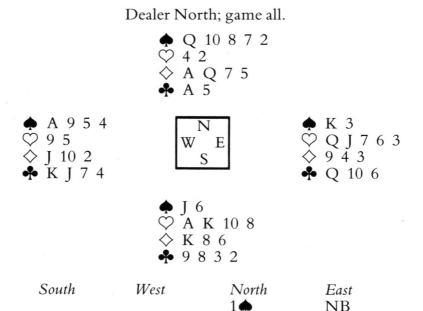

South	West	North	East
		1♠	NB
2NT	NB	3NT(1)	NB
NB	NB		

(1) A brave effort.

Although West seemed to have a number of useful cards himself, he elected to play for his partner's hand by leading the 9 of hearts. South captured East's jack with the king and led the jack of spades to East's king. Looking at dummy, East did not hesitate: he fired back a small heart, and that was that. South won with the eight and played a second spade to ensure his contract – one spade trick, three hearts, four diamonds and one club. As you will see, a club lead from either side of the table would have given the defence five tricks before declarer could come to nine.

(*c*) You should attack against suit contracts whenever you have something with which to attack. I had to bite my lip to stop myself from quoting this Golden Rule to my partner after the following debacle from rubber bridge.

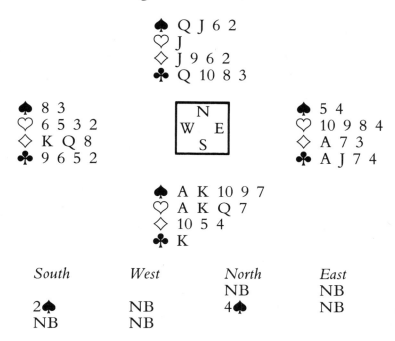

	South	West	North	East
			NB	NB
	2♠	NB	4♠	NB
	NB	NB		

My choice of opening lead from the West hand would be the king of diamonds, and I would not really consider any other card. However, my partner actually selected the 6 of clubs, and we were already under pressure. After some thought, I judged the situation correctly by going up with the ace of clubs, felling South's singleton king. I then switched to the 3 of diamonds, hoping that my partner held something like Q–x and that the declarer would misguess.

My partner won the diamond with the queen, but he then switched studiously to a trump and sent the contract home. I often find that men are reluctant to follow a woman's line of defence, and West was quick to apologise for not following my plan of attack. In my view, however, his biggest mistake on the hand was his negative opening lead. It would require me to have an exceptionally strong holding in clubs for a club lead to be essential, but a diamond lead would certainly be effective if I held the ace or jack opposite, and it might still succeed if I had a worse holding in the suit.

(*d*) You should almost always look for an attacking lead against a small slam contract. The fact that the opponents have stopped in six probably means that the defenders have one certain trick to come; the opening leader's task is to try to develop a second trick before it is too late, and this will often involve making an attacking lead from a holding like K–x–x or Q–x–x. As an example of this principle, here is a deal from the Britain versus France match in the 1977 European Women's Championships in Elsinore, Denmark.

Dealer West; East–West vulnerable.

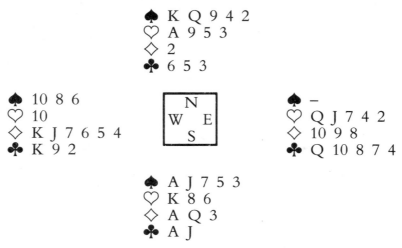

It was not easy for South to keep out of trouble after her opening bid had been raised to game, and both sides reached the poor contract of six spades. Neither West player found the lead which I would have chosen and which would have defeated the contract for certain: the 2 of clubs. When Miss Michelle Brunner was the declarer for Britain, West made the helpful lead of the 10 of hearts. This enabled South to win in dummy with the ace and subsequently lead towards the K–8 to develop a third heart trick and establish dummy's 9 of hearts for a crucial club discard.

At the other table, Miss Nicola Gardener, now Mrs Nicola Smith, found the better opening lead of a small trump. Declarer drew trumps in three rounds and faced the problem of how to develop an extra heart trick for a club discard. If the adverse hearts were 3–3, of course, there would be no problem, and her task would also be simple if either defender held the doubleton Q–J, Q10 or J–10.

There was another slight chance for declarer which became a much stronger possibility when East discarded a heart on the third round of trumps. As East could see four hearts in dummy, this discard was most unlikely to be from a four-card holding. Similarly, East would be unlikely to discard from a three-card heart holding when she would have ten minor-suit cards from which to choose. The early heart discard was therefore quite likely to be from a five-card holding, and the French declarer was quick to realise that, if this was so, there was a 50–50 chance of West's singleton heart being an honour. She therefore cashed the ace of hearts first and was able to establish a third heart trick by force when the singleton ten appeared from West. Plus 980 to France and no swing.

London's Andrew Thompson found an excellent attacking lead against a small slam on the following deal from the 1977 Lederer Memorial Trophy.

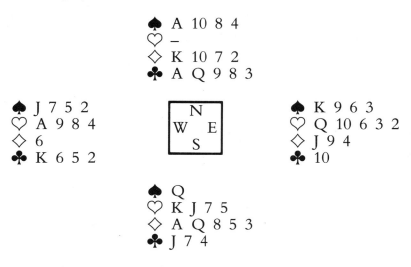

The Scottish international pair, Victor Silverstone and Barnet Shenkin, reached the very reasonable contract of six diamonds by way of a good natural auction:

South	West	North	East
		1♣	NB
1♢	NB	1♠	NB
2♡	NB	4♢	NB
5♣	NB	5♡	NB
6♣	NB	6♢	NB
NB	NB		

In view of the favourable club position, declarer is likely to make 12 tricks fairly comfortably if he is left to his own devices. However, this particular declarer was certainly not permitted to test the clubs in comfort. Andrew Thompson found the excellent lead of the 2 of clubs at trick one and, fearing a singleton club on his left, Shenkin thought for a very long time, even by his standards, before going up with dummy's ace. The 3–1 trump break now left South no scope for recovery, and he ended up with only 11 tricks.

(*e*) The need for an attacking lead against a suit contract is greatest when all seems lost: that is, when you know that everything will break kindly for declarer and that he is likely to have a fairly comfortable ride to his contract unless you can pull off some kind of coup.

The following deal occurred at the rubber bridge table, and I am pleased to say that I held the West cards.

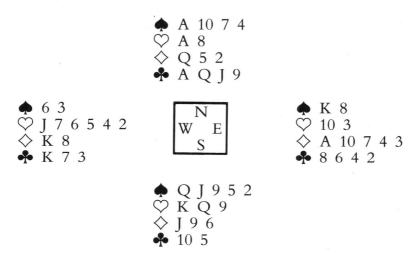

I surveyed my hand with increasing gloom as the auction proceeded:

South	West	North	East
		1♣	NB
1♠	NB	3♠	NB
4♠	NB	NB	NB

Everything seemed likely to go well for South. I knew that the trumps were breaking no worse than 3–2, and I knew from my holding in clubs that it would be a simple task for declarer to develop dummy's first suit. The time had therefore come to attack with what I call the 'desperation' lead of the king of diamonds. When this held, a diamond to the ace and a third-round ruff gave us the first three tricks, and my delighted partner still had the king of spades to come.

PASSIVE LEADS

While I am a determined advocate of attacking leads whenever possible, even I have to admit that there are certain situations in which it is more prudent to make a passive lead and not risk giving anything away. It will probably be helpful if I run through the most common of these situations in this section.

(*a*) Against a no trump contract, it is generally best to make a passive lead when you have a poor hand containing no worthwhile suit. A 'passive' lead in this context really means, of course, that you are hoping to develop tricks in your partner's hand rather than in your own. Here is a spectacular example of an opening lead of this nature from the 1981 Challenge Match between the House of Lords and the House of Commons.

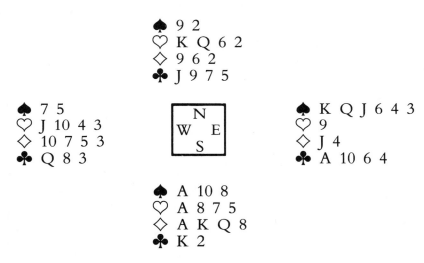

```
                    ♠ 9 2
                    ♡ K Q 6 2
                    ◇ 9 6 2
                    ♣ J 9 7 5

    ♠ 7 5              N              ♠ K Q J 6 4 3
    ♡ J 10 4 3      W     E          ♡ 9
    ◇ 10 7 5 3         S             ◇ J 4
    ♣ Q 8 3                          ♣ A 10 6 4

                    ♠ A 10 8
                    ♡ A 8 7 5
                    ◇ A K Q 8
                    ♣ K 2
```

When the House of Commons team held the North–South cards, Mrs Sally Oppenheim became the declarer in 3NT after the following auction:

South	West	North	East
2NT	NB	3NT(1)	NB
NB	NB		

(1) North clearly has the values for game, but most tournament players would use the Baron Convention in this situation. A bid of three clubs would request the opener to bid his four-card suits in ascending order, and the 4–4 heart fit would come to light after the auction:

South	West	North	East
2NT	NB	3♣	NB
3♢	NB	3♡	NB
4♡	NB	NB	NB

Four hearts would have been a better contract on the North–South hands, but 3NT had chances – that is, until the Duke of Atholl, who has established quite a reputation for dynamic opening leads, found the devastating shot of the 7 of spades. Against this inspired attack, Sally Oppenheim had no chance at all, and she ended up with only six tricks.

(*b*) Against a suit contract, it may be best to make a passive trump lead if you have unattractive holdings from which to lead in the side suits. However, I strongly recommend that you should make this variety of trump lead only as a last resort, for you are effectively giving the declarer time to play the hand along the lines which he chooses. Moreover, it must be borne in mind that an expert declarer may draw inferences about the overall nature of your hand if he suspects that you have made a passive trump lead. Here, for example, is the Danish expert Alex Koltscheff in action when I played with him in Deauville in 1981.

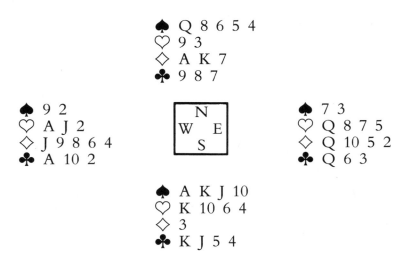

♠ Q 8 6 5 4
♡ 9 3
♢ A K 7
♣ 9 8 7

♠ 9 2
♡ A J 2
♢ J 9 8 6 4
♣ A 10 2

N
W   E
S

♠ 7 3
♡ Q 8 7 5
♢ Q 10 5 2
♣ Q 6 3

♠ A K J 10
♡ K 10 6 4
♢ 3
♣ K J 5 4

Koltscheff opened one spade on the South hand, and I raised to game without further ado. The opening lead was a trump, which my partner regarded as a sure indication that West held unsupported honours in the side suits and was anxious not to give away a trick on the opening lead. South won in the closed hand, cashed two top diamonds and ruffed a diamond in hand. He then crossed to dummy with the queen of spades and ran the 9 of clubs, losing to West's 10. West was already end-played. He exited with a diamond, and declarer ruffed in dummy, discarding a heart from the closed hand, and ran the 8 of clubs, drawing West's ace.

West was powerless. He could see that with the defenders' clubs breaking 3–3, declarer would be able to discard a heart from dummy on the 13th club. West therefore played the ace and another heart, but South won the second round with the king to bring home his game contract on a hand on which a lesser declarer might well have lost four tricks.

(c) If your hand presents no obvious opening lead, your choice of passive lead may have to be made by the simple process of eliminating all the clearly bad leads. Michael Wolach defeated a vulnerable game at rubber bridge recently by doing just this.

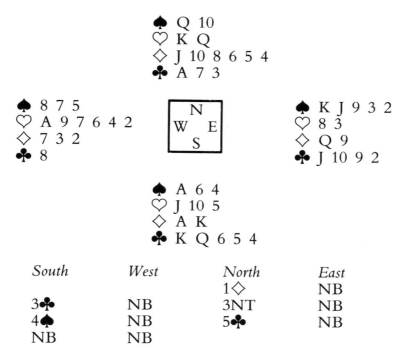

♠ Q 10
♡ K Q
◇ J 10 8 6 5 4
♣ A 7 3

♠ 8 7 5
♡ A 9 7 6 4 2
◇ 7 3 2
♣ 8

N
W　E
S

♠ K J 9 3 2
♡ 8 3
◇ Q 9
♣ J 10 9 2

♠ A 6 4
♡ J 10 5
◇ A K
♣ K Q 6 5 4

South	West	North	East
		1◇	NB
3♣	NB	3NT	NB
4♠	NB	5♣	NB
NB	NB		

To lead the ace of hearts would squander West's only entry prematurely; to lead the singleton trump might kill his partner's likely trick in the suit; and to lead a diamond through dummy's long suit would be to do declarer's work for him. Michael Wolach therefore tried to develop a third trick for the defence by leading a spade at trick one, and this proved to be the only lead to defeat the contract.

(*d*) It is normally best to make a passive lead when you know that the hand is going to play badly for the declarer and when you are therefore anxious to avoid giving a trick away on the opening lead. For example, suppose you hold the following hand:

West
♠ Q 9 8 4
♡ 10 9 7 5
♢ K 7 5 2
♣ 4

and you hear the bidding proceed as follows:

South	West	North	East
NB	NB	1♣	NB
1♠	NB	2♠	NB
2NT	NB	4♠	NB
NB	NB		

You know that the opponents have nothing to spare, for South's hand is limited by his original pass and North's hand is limited by his second-round raise to just two spades; you know that the trumps are breaking 4–1; and you know that dummy's club suit is doomed to break badly, with all the defenders' strength in the suit lying *over* dummy's holding. Your conclusion should therefore be that, left to his own devices, South will probably go down in his contract of four spades. With this in mind, you should select the lead which is least likely to give away a trick, and the essentially passive lead of the 10 of hearts is the recommended choice from this holding.

9 Getting the Message

Defensive signalling is a subject which all aspiring partnerships must discuss thoroughly and agree upon; they will find that sound, accurate defence is virtually impossible unless they make good use of their small and comparatively worthless cards in order to convey vital information about their distribution and/or the whereabouts of their high cards.

The meaning of defensive signals normally varies depending on whether they are being made on declarer's lead or on partner's lead. I therefore propose to cover each of these two topics in turn.

SIGNALS ON DECLARER'S LEAD

When he is following to a suit led by dummy or declarer, a defender should normally play his small cards in an order which has been pre-determined and which will convey valuable information about distribution to his partner. The standard method in this country is to play those small cards in ascending order to show an odd number of cards in that suit, and to 'peter' (play high–low) in order to show an even number.

There are one or two points which I would like to make on the subject of distributional signals in a suit being played by the declarer:

(*a*) Never peter with an honour which is not part of a sequence. To do so might well concede a trick or, at best, improve declarer's communications between the two hands.

(*b*) Never peter if the information which you are conveying will help declarer more than your partner. I have, for example, seen some inexperienced East–West players petering studiously in this kind of situation:

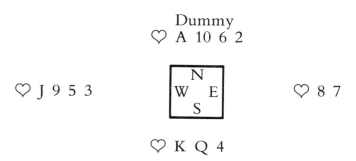

```
              Dummy
           ♡ A 10 6 2
                 ┌───┐
                 │ N │
♡ J 9 5 3        │W  E│        ♡ 8 7
                 │ S │
                 └───┘
           ♡ K Q 4
```

If East and West both peter when South cashes the king and queen of hearts, they must not be too disappointed if their opponent takes a good view by finessing the 10 on the third round of the suit.

(*c*) Subject to the proviso which I made in (*b*), you should stick to your agreed method of signalling whenever you believe that your partner might be interested to receive the information. There is nothing more galling to a partner than to make a reasoned defence based on the data which you appear to have given him, only to find that you have elected not to bother to signal on this particular hand. I had some sympathy for the East player on the following deal from the final of the 1980 European Pairs Championship.

Dealer South; love all.

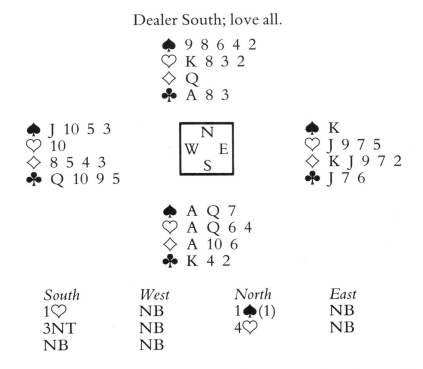

	South	West	North	East
	1♡	NB	1♠(1)	NB
	3NT	NB	4♡	NB
	NB	NB		

(1) The English style would be to make an immediate limit raise to three hearts on this eight-loser hand. The actual sequence which the French player in the North seat adopted would normally show both a better spade suit and a better hand.

West led a diamond, and declarer, the French expert Leon Tintner, captured the king with the ace, ruffed a diamond in dummy and led a spade to the king and ace. West should have begun to peter by playing the 5 of spades on this trick, thereby showing an even number of cards in the suit. When he absentmindedly contributed the 3, East was led to believe that West held five spades and South two, and this caused him to go wrong in the subsequent play.

After winning with the ace of spades, South ruffed his last diamond in dummy and led a second spade towards the closed hand. East was anxious to lead a round of trumps and, believing that he would be capturing declarer's queen of spades, he ruffed the second spade. When it transpired that he had ruffed South's losing spade with his trump trick, there was nothing East could do to recover. South eventually established dummy's fifth spade for a club discard, and +450 gave the French pair an excellent match-point score.

(*d*) Do not forget that, on occasions, it will be more important to show partner that you have a sequence of high cards than that you have an odd or even number of cards in the suit. Unless you maintain this degree of flexibility in your signalling system, you will not be able to emulate this brilliant defence found by US stars Edgar Kaplan and Norman Kay:

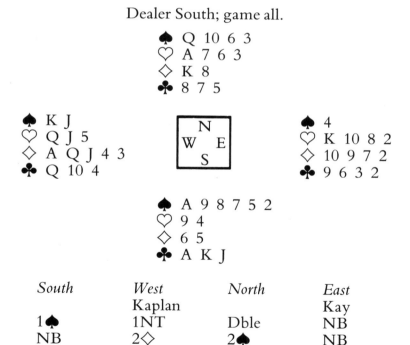

Dealer South; game all.

```
                    ♠ Q 10 6 3
                    ♡ A 7 6 3
                    ◇ K 8
                    ♣ 8 7 5
♠ K J                   N              ♠ 4
♡ Q J 5          W         E          ♡ K 10 8 2
◇ A Q J 4 3            S              ◇ 10 9 7 2
♣ Q 10 4                              ♣ 9 6 3 2
                    ♠ A 9 8 7 5 2
                    ♡ 9 4
                    ◇ 6 5
                    ♣ A K J
```

South	West	North	East
	Kaplan		Kay
1♠	1NT	Dble	NB
NB	2◇	2♠	NB
4♠	NB	NB	NB

West led the queen of hearts. Declarer ducked in dummy, and East overtook with the king and switched to a club. South went up with the ace and played a diamond towards dummy's king. Kaplan inserted the jack, and the co-operative East dropped the 10 under the king, thereby promising the 9. Declarer now cashed the ace of hearts, ruffed a heart and exited with his remaining diamond. West allowed this to run to his partner's 9, and a club continuation by East defeated the contract by one trick.

As you will see, it takes a very good co-operative defence to prevent West from being end-played on this deal; at the other table, in fact, Kaplan and Kay's team-mates succeeded in making four spades without too much difficulty.

SIGNALS ON PARTNER'S LEAD

While almost everybody agrees that signals on a lead made by declarer or dummy should show length, there is not the same measure of agreement over the meaning of signals on partner's lead. There are, in fact, two distinct schools of thought and two perfectly playable methods: Attitude Signals and Length Signals.

Attitude Signals

Advocates of attitude signals suggest that your first signal on partner's lead should indicate your reaction thereto: if you are keen for him to continue the suit at the earliest possible opportunity, you should play the highest card which you can afford; if your feeling is that partner should try elsewhere for honey, you should contribute your lowest card.

You will notice that I stressed above that you should signal encouragement by following *with the highest card which you can afford*. Thereby hangs a salutary tale from the final stages of the 1978 Gold Cup competition, in a crucial match between Posner and Pencharz.

Dealer South, East–West vulnerable.

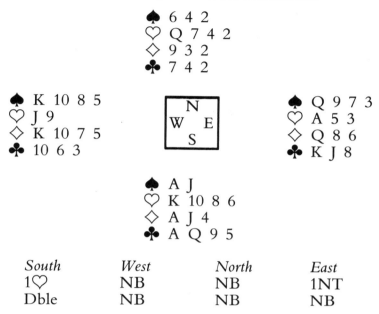

	South	West	North	East
	1♡	NB	NB	1NT
	Dble	NB	NB	NB

South led the 5 of clubs to East's 8. Declarer now led the queen of spades from his hand, and South went in with the ace and found an excellent switch to the king of hearts. This was allowed to hold the trick, and South continued with the 10 of hearts, which was covered by the jack, queen and ace. This splendid defence had paved the way for a penalty of 500, for the defenders were now in a position to cash one spade, one diamond, three hearts and three clubs, when North won the fourth round of hearts and pushed a club through.

Unfortunately, however, North had shown excessive exuberance on the first round of hearts. He had extravagantly squandered the 7 of hearts in order to signal his approval for his partner's switch, and the result was that he could no longer gain the lead with a heart to return a club through declarer's tenace. What might well have been +500 to Pencharz therefore became +180 to Posner.

If you can afford your highest card in order to signal your enthusiasm for partner's lead, you should play it. This applies particularly when you have a sequence of honours, and the East–West pair were found wanting on the following fascinating hand from rubber bridge.

Dealer South; game all.

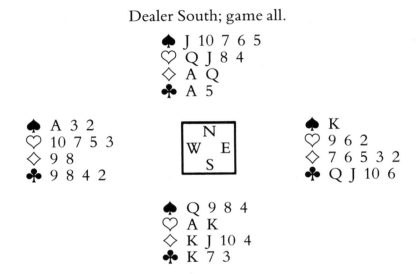

Sir Rodney Smith, the world-famous surgeon who is now Lord Smith of Marlow, was partnering the late Karel Stepanek, the actor. Stepanek displayed his characteristic optimism in the following auction.

South	West	North	East
Smith		Stepanek	
1NT	NB	2♣(1)	NB
2♠	NB	4♢(2)	NB
4♡	NB	6♠	NB
NB	NB		

(1) Stayman, asking the opener to show a four-card major suit.

(2) An advance cue bid, agreeing spades as trumps.

This spirited auction left Sir Rodney Smith with the difficult task of making a slam missing the ace and king of trumps, but he found a neat deceptive play. West led the 9 of clubs, won in dummy by the ace. East played the 10 of clubs as an encouraging card, but it would have clarified matters for his unfortunate partner if he had contributed the queen of clubs, thereby denying the king. South immediately played the ace and queen of diamonds, overtaking with the king, and led the jack of diamonds with the air of a man who was attempting to discard dummy's losing club. West ruffed low, and declarer over-ruffed in dummy, cross back to hand with a heart and repeated the process by leading the 10 of diamonds. West once again obliged by ruffing low, and declarer over-ruffed and led a round of trumps, crashing the ace and king together. 'Well played, partner', beamed Stepanek, 'I knew you would make it!'.

There is no doubt that attitude signals can work very well on certain hands. Here is a good example from the Pairs Championship at the 1984 Cannes Bridge Festival.

Dealer South; North–South vulnerable.

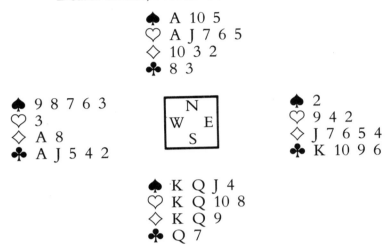

South became the declarer in four hearts and, seeking the third-round ruff which would defeat the contract at trick four, West led the ace of diamonds. If East–West had been playing length signals, East would have contributed the 4 in order to show an odd number of diamonds and West would not have known whether or not to continue. As it was, the partnership favoured attitude signals, and East's 4 of diamonds suggested that a switch would be welcomed. West therefore tried the effect of the ace and another club, and he and his partner earned themselves an excellent match-point score by holding declarer to just ten tricks.

The other principal advantage of attitude signals is their flexibility, for they make it possible to direct the defence by means of the tactical use of one's small cards. Here is an interesting example from the Swiss teams event in the Romanian International Bridge Festival in Mamaia, 1981.

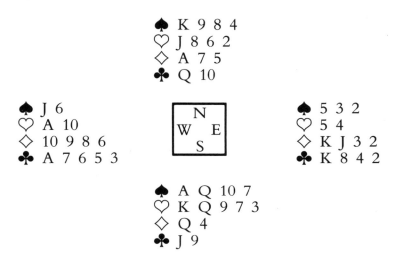

At my table, I opened one heart on the South hand and quickly found myself in the very poor contract of four hearts. With no discards immediately available, I was almost certain to lose one heart, one diamond and two clubs, but help was at hand. West led the 10 of diamonds, and I ducked in dummy and lost to East's king. It was now not at all clear to East that he should switch to a club, and he exited passively with a second diamond. This enabled me to win with the queen, cross to dummy with a spade and discard one of my clubs on the ace of diamonds, thereby restricting my losers to one heart, one diamond and one club.

At the other table, our opponents reached the slightly superior contract of four spades. This will make if the declarer is given sufficient time to discard one of dummy's clubs on the fifth heart, but our Romanian team-mates made no mistake: they defeated the contract by means of a shrewd piece of signalling. West led the ace of clubs, on which East contributed the 2, discouraging a club continuation and ostensibly showing a poor holding in the suit. West immediately switched to a diamond, and this meant that South had absolutely no chance of scrambling home.

Length Signals

While attitude signals are used by a large number of expert partnerships, and are certainly recommended for use by comparative beginners at the game, I actually prefer to play an alternative signalling method – length or distributional signals. Under this method, the third player signals on his partner's lead in exactly the same way as he does on declarer's lead, playing his lowest card to show an odd number of cards in the suit and beginning a peter if he has an even number.

Length signals are designed to give partner a count of the suit and therefore a contribution towards a count of the entire hand. I personally regard this as much more important than trying to guide partner towards the correct defence: after all, he has seen dummy and he has heard the bidding, and he should be able to build up a pretty clear picture of the unseen hands.

Here is an interesting illustration of the merits of length signals. I have composed a full layout based on the first problem in Victor Mollo's excellent book, *I Challenge You*.

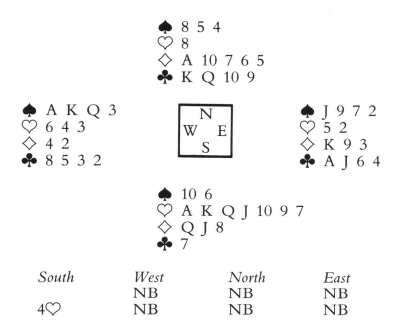

	♠ 8 5 4	
	♡ 8	
	◇ A 10 7 6 5	
	♣ K Q 10 9	

♠ A K Q 3		♠ J 9 7 2
♡ 6 4 3	N	♡ 5 2
◇ 4 2	W E	◇ K 9 3
♣ 8 5 3 2	S	♣ A J 6 4

	♠ 10 6	
	♡ A K Q J 10 9 7	
	◇ Q J 8	
	♣ 7	

South	*West*	*North*	*East*
	NB	NB	NB
4♡	NB	NB	NB

Victor Mollo's challenge to his readers was to make four hearts, without seeing the East–West hands, after West had started with the ace, king and queen of spades. His solution was as follows. Once West has produced the three top spades, you know for certain that he cannot also hold the ace of clubs, or he would have opened the bidding. The winning play is therefore to ruff the third round of spades with the 9 of hearts and play a club to dummy's 9. If West has the jack of clubs, the 9 will draw East's ace and the king and queen of clubs will provide discards for your losing diamonds. If East has the jack of clubs, dummy's 9 will lose to the jack, but you will be able to use the 8 of hearts as an entry to dummy in order to lead the king of clubs for a ruffing finesse. Having ruffed out East's ace of clubs, you can draw trumps and cross to dummy with the ace of diamonds in order to discard your two diamond losers on the established clubs.

This is a very neat problem, but I would not give many marks to the defenders for their performance on this hand. When West cashed the ace and king of spades, East should have followed with the 7 and 2, showing an even number of cards in the suit. Since South was most unlikely to have opened four hearts if he also held J–9–x–x of spades, West would realise that the third spade would not stand up. A diamond switch at trick three would then establish a fourth trick for the defence.

While I prefer playing length signals and giving partner a count as a general rule, there are a few situations in which it makes good sense to switch to attitude signals. I am always perfectly happy to give encouraging or discouraging signals in the following exceptional circumstances:

(*a*) When partner's lead of the king is ducked and he does not know whether or not he is being lured into a Bath Coup. For example:

North
Dummy
♢ A 4 2

♢ K lead   *East*
                                                    ♢ J 8 3

If declarer ducks the king of diamonds lead in this situation, it will set your partner's mind at rest if you encourage with the 8. He will not otherwise be certain that it is safe to continue the suit. However:

North
Dummy
♢ 10 4 2

♢ K lead   *East*
                                                    ♢ J 8 3

If partner leads the king of diamonds in this position, I make my normal distributional signal of the three, suggesting an odd number of cards in the suit. If the king of diamonds is ducked, West will know that I have either the ace or the jack and that it is therefore safe to continue; if declarer had both the ace and jack of diamonds, he would win the first trick in order to ensure two tricks in the suit.

(*b*) When partner leads an ace in a situation in which the defending side clearly have to cash their tricks in a hurry. This will normally occur in the middle of the hand when it is clear to all that declarer has a long suit on which he is threatening to discard his losers. However, it can also occur at trick one if, for example, declarer has opened with a gambling 3NT bid based on a long, solid minor suit.

In the same way, of course, it is essential to make exceptions to the general rule when your basic method involves the use of attitude signals. The most common of these exceptions arises where it is vital for partner to know whether you have a singleton or doubleton in the suit which he has led. Consider, for example, the following instructive deal from a pairs event at the Vienna Bridge Festival in February 1981.

Dealer East; North–South vulnerable.

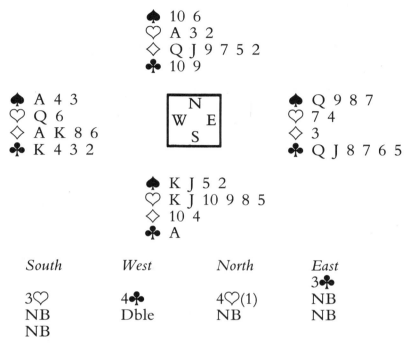

```
                    ♠ 10 6
                    ♡ A 3 2
                    ◇ Q J 9 7 5 2
                    ♣ 10 9

  ♠ A 4 3            ┌─────────┐        ♠ Q 9 8 7
  ♡ Q 6             │    N    │        ♡ 7 4
  ◇ A K 8 6         │ W     E │        ◇ 3
  ♣ K 4 3 2         │    S    │        ♣ Q J 8 7 6 5
                     └─────────┘

                    ♠ K J 5 2
                    ♡ K J 10 9 8 5
                    ◇ 10 4
                    ♣ A
```

South	West	North	East
			3♣
3♡	4♣	4♡(1)	NB
NB	Dble	NB	NB
NB			

(1) I hoped that the vulnerability might persuade East–West to sacrifice in five clubs but they would not take the bait.

This hand is a good illustration of the progress which the top Hungarian players have made in recent years. The Hungarian player in the West seat led the ace of diamonds against four hearts doubled. Since he knew that his partner would have started a peter if he held a doubleton diamond, West knew for certain that East's 3 of diamonds was a singleton. He therefore made the key play of leading a small diamond for his partner to ruff at the second trick, and the contract was now doomed to defeat: there was no way in which declarer could avoid the loss of two spade tricks.

My partner and I scored very few match-points for conceding −200 on the North–South cards. Several defenders at other tables allowed South to make ten tricks in heart contracts, and several other East–West pairs 'sacrificed' in five clubs doubled.

Suit Preference Signals

As well as length signals and occasional attitude signals, my regular
partners and I always include suit preference signals as part of our
defensive armoury.

Suit preference signals are used widely and effectively in certain
situations: for example, when you are giving partner a ruff and are
anxious to indicate which of the two remaining suits he should return
in order to give you the lead for another ruff. Here is an interesting
deal with this theme from the 1982 Life Masters Pairs.

Dealer West; game all.

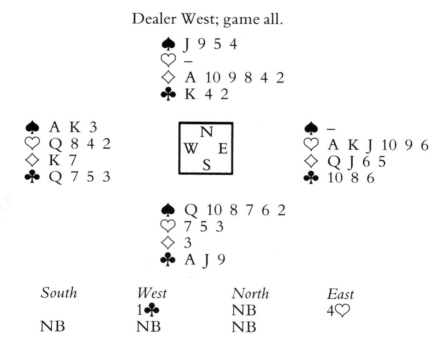

	South	West	North	East
		1♣	NB	4♡
	NB	NB	NB	

South led his singleton diamond against the final contract of four
hearts, and North won with the ace and returned the 2 of diamonds
for South to ruff. A spade switch at this point would have conceded
the contract, and the actual switch to the ace and another club
collected a modest +100.

In order to bring in +200 and most of the match-points, South
should switch to the *jack* of clubs, thereby enabling the defenders to
collect three club tricks. In my view, he should find this defence for
two reasons. First, North's return of the 2 of diamonds was a clear
suit preference signal, calling for the lower of the two side suits; and
second, it was most unlikely that East held the king of clubs. The play
to the first two tricks marked East with ◇Q–J–x–x; if he also held
the king of clubs he would not have been in such a hurry to jump to

four hearts.

Here is another example of unmistakable suit preference signals, this time from the 1978 Gold Cup competition.

Dealer South; game all.

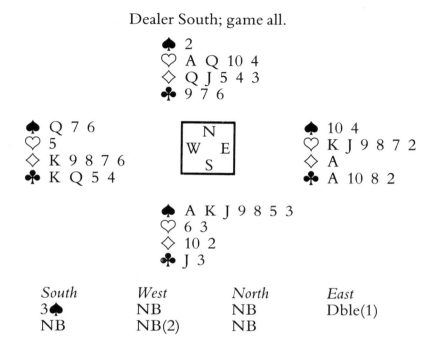

South	West	North	East
3♠	NB	NB	Dble(1)
NB	NB(2)	NB	

(1) A take-out double, guaranteeing nothing more than a reasonable opening hand.

(2) West, Bill Pencharz, judged well by deciding to try for a penalty from three spades doubled.

The defence was perfect. West led the king of clubs, and East, Raymond Brock, overtook with the ace, cashed the ace of diamonds and returned the 8 of clubs. West won with the queen and now switched to his singleton heart. In view of West's failure to lead a heart originally, declarer did not suspect that this was a singleton, and he inserted the queen from dummy. East won with the king and returned the jack of hearts. This unnecessarily high card was an obvious suit preference signal asking for a diamond return, and West co-operated by ruffing the second heart and returning the 9 of diamonds for East to ruff. Another heart return, as requested by the unnecessarily high diamond, now promoted West's queen of spades into another trump trick. This excellent defence by Pencharz and Brock brought them +800 on a board on which they could not even make a game contract.

In ruffing situations of this kind, suit preference signals are clearly understood. The same is certainly not true of suit preference signals on partner's lead, and even quite experienced defenders do not always agree about which signals are which and when suit preference messages can be safely relayed without fear of their being misinterpreted. As I see it, the cards which you play on partner's lead can be used to convey suit preference messages provided that the following conditions are met:

(*a*) You are not attempting to win the trick.

(*b*) Partner cannot be hoping to receive a length signal.

(*c*) Partner cannot be expecting to receive an attitude signal.

(*d*) It is clear that a switch is essential.

As long as these four conditions are fulfilled, suit preference signals can be employed in situations where length or attitude signals would normally apply – and this includes situations arising at the first trick. I have never understood why so many experts maintain that you cannot use suit preference signals at trick one, and it does not make sense to me to ignore any opportunity to give partner an immediate guide to his next move.

Tony Priday suggested in his contribution to the excellent series of Bols Bridge Tips that there are often situations in which the opening leader should attempt to hold the first trick; if it can be combined with a suit preference signal from partner, this strategy can sometimes work extremely well. Here is an interesting example from the 1982 Juan-les-Pins Festival.

Dealer East; game all.

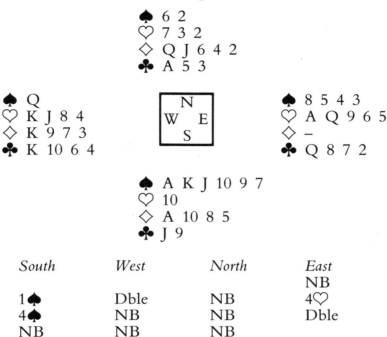

♠ 6 2
♡ 7 3 2
♢ Q J 6 4 2
♣ A 5 3

♠ Q
♡ K J 8 4
♢ K 9 7 3
♣ K 10 6 4

♠ 8 5 4 3
♡ A Q 9 6 5
♢ –
♣ Q 8 7 2

♠ A K J 10 9 7
♡ 10
♢ A 10 8 5
♣ J 9

South	West	North	East
			NB
1♠	Dble	NB	4♡
4♠	NB	NB	Dble
NB	NB	NB	

In order to preserve flexibility between the two defenders' hands, West leads the king of hearts against four spades doubled. If he is alert, East will contribute the queen of hearts at the first trick – a clear suit preference signal calling for the high-ranking of the two side suits. West switches obediently to a diamond, East ruffs and returns a club, and the contract goes one down, the defenders taking one heart, one diamond, one club and a diamond ruff. It is interesting to note that four spades cannot be defeated if West leads a *small* heart at trick one.

10   A Switch in Time

I have always regarded defence as the most difficult aspect of our difficult game. The basic reason is, of course, that whereas the declarer has the advantage of being able to see and manipulate all his side's 26 cards, a defender is only permitted to see his own and one of the opponents' hands. He therefore has to try to build up a mental picture of the two unseen holdings as quickly as possible, drawing inferences from the bidding, from the opening lead, from the way the declarer has tackled the play and from defensive signals transmitted by his partner.

One of the questions which beginners and inexperienced players always find extremely difficult is when to get busy in the defence and when to adopt a purely passive role and leave the declarer to his own devices. As a general rule, I would suggest that it is usually best not to get too active as a defender, particularly when you can tell that the cards are not lying favourably for the declarer. I think it was the American expert Charles Goren who estimated that defenders give away an average of half a trick every time they switch to a new suit, and there is nothing which I enjoy more when I am playing a hand than to be opposed by two 'busy' defenders who can be relied upon to switch athletically from suit to suit. I have noticed particularly that defenders tend to become too active when they have got off to a bad start with their opening lead. Even if you have given away a trick with your opening salvo, it is often best to persevere with the same suit next time, especially when the declarer's communications between his two hands are poor: to switch to another suit will often do the declarer's work for him and present him with a second trick to go with the one which he was given by the first lead.

My general rule for defenders is: play passively unless there is a very good reason for not doing so. The most compelling reason for switching to a new suit is that it is the only realistic hope of defeating the contract, and it will often be worthwhile at teams or rubber bridge to take a slight chance in an effort to beat a contract which looks like being made if the declarer is allowed to continue under his own steam. My partner took this kind of chance on the following deal from the Deauville Bridge Festival.

Dealer North; North–South vulnerable.

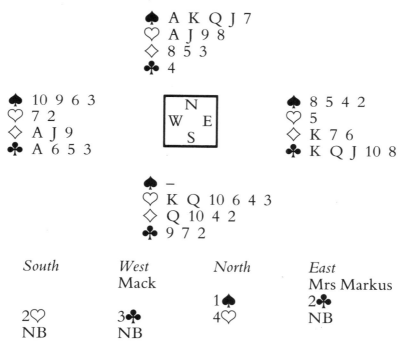

♠ A K Q J 7
♡ A J 9 8
◇ 8 5 3
♣ 4

♠ 10 9 6 3
♡ 7 2
◇ A J 9
♣ A 6 5 3

♠ 8 5 4 2
♡ 5
◇ K 7 6
♣ K Q J 10 8

♠ —
♡ K Q 10 6 4 3
◇ Q 10 4 2
♣ 9 7 2

South	West Mack	North	East Mrs Markus
		1♠	2♣
2♡	3♣	4♡	NB
NB	NB		

David Mack led the ace of clubs against four hearts and, despite a false-card of the 9 from the declarer, he found the winning defence in a flash. Mack realised that, unless the defence got busy, South was likely to make at least 11 tricks: five hearts, five spades and one club ruff in dummy. In order to defeat the contract, my partner had to find me with the king of diamonds, or possibly the king of hearts plus the queen or 10 of diamonds. He therefore switched to the 9 of diamonds at trick two, and we took the first four tricks to defeat a contract which was made at several tables.

The dramatic switch on this next deal was found by my dear friend Andor Keleti, who was a member of the legendary Hungarian team of the 1930s and who died in 1983 at the age of 82. This hand is from the 1934 European Championships in Vienna. It occurred during the match between Hungary and the Netherlands, who at that time were two of the strongest teams in Europe.

Dealer North; North–South vulnerable.

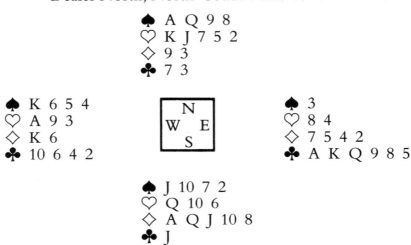

```
              ♠ A Q 9 8
              ♡ K J 7 5 2
              ◇ 9 3
              ♣ 7 3
 ♠ K 6 5 4        N         ♠ 3
 ♡ A 9 3      W       E     ♡ 8 4
 ◇ K 6           S         ◇ 7 5 4 2
 ♣ 10 6 4 2                 ♣ A K Q 9 8 5
              ♠ J 10 7 2
              ♡ Q 10 6
              ◇ A Q J 10 8
              ♣ J
```

When Hungary held the North–South cards, they bid and made four spades to score +620. At the other table:

South	West	North	East
	Leitner		Keleti
		NB	NB
1♦	NB	1♡	2♣
NB	2NT(1)	Dble	NB
NB	3♣	NB	NB
3♦	NB	NB	NB

(1) This was a good bid by West. He succeeded in shutting out the opponents' spade fit while at the same time paving the way for a five club sacrifice, should it have become necessary.

Three diamonds proved to be the wrong contract, and Keleti defeated it in a matter of seconds. Having won the first round of clubs with the queen, he calculated that his partner was likely to have two quick tricks in the red suits in order to justify his bid of 2NT. This reasoning made it simple to defeat the contract. Keleti switched to a spade, straight into the teeth of dummy's tenace. South won in the closed hand and played the ace and another diamond. West won with the king and gave his partner a spade ruff; a heart to the ace and a second spade ruff then defeated the contract by one trick. It also earned Andor Keleti a round of applause from the enthusiastic audience.

Sometimes a defender has the problem of finding not only the right suit to which to switch, but also the right card in the right suit. The following deal from the Cannes Bridge Festival shows a splendid defence by the Polish champions Ostrowski and Wolny. It all hinges on a devastating switch by East.

Dealer South; North–South vulnerable.

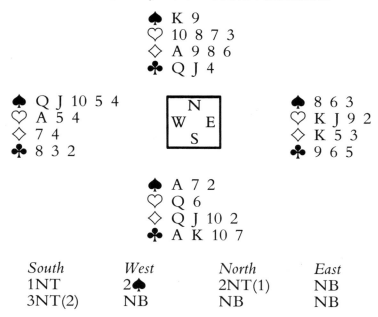

	♠ K 9	
	♡ 10 8 7 3	
	◇ A 9 8 6	
	♣ Q J 4	

♠ Q J 10 5 4
♡ A 5 4
◇ 7 4
♣ 8 3 2

♠ 8 6 3
♡ K J 9 2
◇ K 5 3
♣ 9 6 5

♠ A 7 2
♡ Q 6
◇ Q J 10 2
♣ A K 10 7

South	*West*	*North*	*East*
1NT	2♠	2NT(1)	NB
3NT(2)	NB	NB	NB

(1) Forcing, and asking South to describe his hand further.
(2) Denying four hearts.

West led the queen of spades against 3NT. Declarer won in dummy with the king, hoping thereby to conceal the whereabouts of the ace, and crossed to the closed hand with the ace of clubs in order to take the diamond finesse.

Wolny was not fooled into returning a spade after winning with the king of diamonds. He knew that South must have the ace of spades in order to justify his rebid of 3NT; furthermore, the play of the clubs at trick two made it almost certain that South had A–K–x –x in the suit. East therefore knew that the only chance of defeating 3NT lay in cashing four heart tricks. South had to have the queen of hearts for his strong no trump opening bid. The only hope was that the queen was doubleton, and East found the brilliant shot of cashing the king of hearts and continuing with a second heart to the queen and ace. This created a tenace position over dummy's 10–8, and defeated the contract by one trick when Ostrowski was able to return a third round of hearts.

Britain's John Collings found a similarly devastating switch on the following board from a key match in the final stages of the Gold Cup, the national knockout teams championship.

Dealer East; game all.

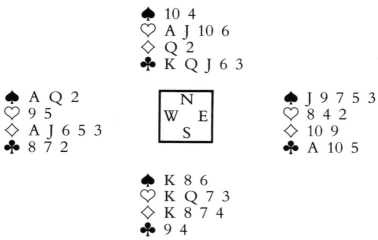

♠ 10 4
♥ A J 10 6
♦ Q 2
♣ K Q J 6 3

♠ A Q 2
♥ 9 5
♦ A J 6 5 3
♣ 8 7 2

♠ J 9 7 5 3
♥ 8 4 2
♦ 10 9
♣ A 10 5

♠ K 8 6
♥ K Q 7 3
♦ K 8 7 4
♣ 9 4

The bidding was the same at both tables:

South	West	North	East
			NB
NB	1♦	2♣	NB
2NT	NB	3NT	NB
NB	NB		

When Bill Pencharz's team held the North–South cards, West led the 5 of diamonds. Declarer won with the queen in dummy and embarked on the club suit. John Collings, who was in the East chair, captured the king of clubs with the ace and found the brilliant play of switching to the jack of spades. He reasoned quite correctly that South's intermediate cards in diamonds might well be strong enough to give him a certain second trick in the suit; more important, he reasoned that even if West's diamond suit was sufficiently good to restrict South to one trick, say A–J–8–5–3, the declarer would certainly not oblige by covering the 10 with the king. The best chance of defeating the contract therefore lay in picking up three spade tricks, and the jack of spades had the desired effect. At the other table, East rather woodenly returned a diamond after winning with the ace of clubs. Declarer covered with the king, and he could no longer be defeated.

John Collings seems to specialise in finding sparkling switches at just the right moment. Here he is in action with Paul Hackett at the Caransa–Philip Morris Teams Tournament in Amsterdam.

Dealer North; game all.

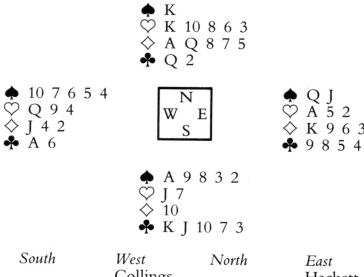

South	West Collings	North	East Hackett
		1♡	NB
1♠	NB	2◇	NB
2NT	NB	3◇	NB
3♡	NB	3NT	NB
NB	NB		

Collings led the 7 of spades against the final contract of 3NT. Under their defensive methods, this showed a suit in which he had little interest, the principle of these so-called 'attitude leads' being the lower the card led, the better the suit.

Declarer won the first trick in dummy and led the queen of clubs, which was allowed to hold the trick. A second round of clubs lost to West's ace, and Collings now found the killing switch of the jack of diamonds, pinning South's singleton 10.

Declarer finessed the queen of diamonds from dummy, and Hackett won with the king and completed South's misery by switching to a small heart, which went to the 7, 9 and 10. Declarer was now securely locked in dummy, and he had to exit by playing the ace and another diamond. East won with the 9 and played back the jack of spades. When South foolishly allowed this to hold, there was no escape for him: Hackett threw dummy in with his last diamond, and the defenders still had to come to two heart tricks. Two down and +200 for East–West, and a useful swing for them when their team-mates at the other table managed to stay in a safe part-score on the North–South cards.

My next example of a spectacular switch to the only card to defeat the contract occurred when I was making one of my rare appearances in the Gold Cup competition a year or two ago. To my everlasting shame, I have to confess that I failed to find the winning defence when I held the East hand.

Dealer South; North–South vulnerable.

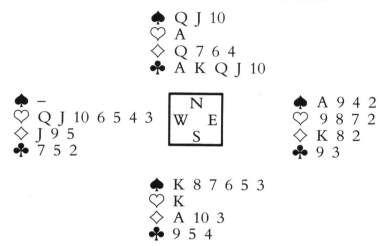

The bidding at my table was as follows:

South	West	North	East
NB(1)	NB(2)	1♣	NB
1♠	NB	3◇(3)	NB
4◇	NB	4NT	NB
5◇	NB	6♠	NB
NB	NB		

(1) The South player at the other table opened one spade on this hand, but I agree with the first-round pass. On this kind of holding, I prefer to wait and listen rather than mislead partner by opening with so few high-card values.

(2) My partner made a strange pass here; I would always open three hearts at favourable vulnerability.

(3) This was an excellent bid by North, who realised that he had the values for game and decided to set about showing his shape on the way.

My partner led the queen of hearts against six spades, and declarer won in dummy with the ace and led the queen of spades, which held the trick. A second round of spades was taken by East's ace, and the crucial stage of the defence had been reached. I decided to play declarer for a singleton club, and I switched to a club in an attempt to nullify dummy's long suit. On reflection, this was quite wrong: if declarer was 6–1–5–1 as I was hoping, he would be able to finesse against my king of diamonds in any case.

At the other table, Clive Hyams found a superior defensive shot. The play began in the same way, but when East won the second spade with the ace, he fired back the king of diamonds. This nailed South in his hand and made it impossible for him to get back to hand in order to draw the outstanding trump. After this sparkling defence, declarer had no chance: he could cross to dummy with the 10 of spades, but the fact that East had only two clubs left South with an unavoidable loser in either trumps or diamonds. Full marks to Master Hyams; none at all to me on that occasion.

The dramatic switches which the expert defenders found on the preceding hands were made because they represented the only realistic chance of defeating the contract. It may also be necessary on occasions to switch in order to dissuade the declarer from pursuing what seems likely to be a winning line of play. The Oxford West player found an excellent defensive play on the following deal from the 1981 'Varsity Match.

Dealer West; love all.

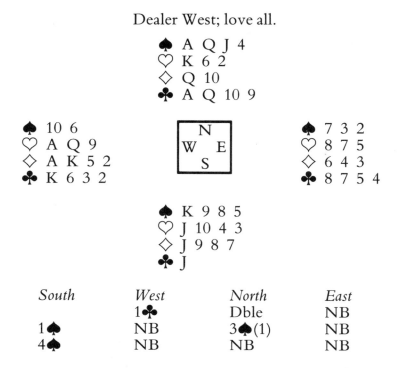

♠ A Q J 4
♡ K 6 2
◇ Q 10
♣ A Q 10 9

♠ 10 6
♡ A Q 9
◇ A K 5 2
♣ K 6 3 2

♠ 7 3 2
♡ 8 7 5
◇ 6 4 3
♣ 8 7 5 4

♠ K 9 8 5
♡ J 10 4 3
◇ J 9 8 7
♣ J

South	West	North	East
	1♣	Dble	NB
1♠	NB	3♠(1)	NB
4♠	NB	NB	NB

(1) I would personally prefer to rebid 1NT at this point, showing a hand which was just too strong for an immediate overcall of 1NT on the previous round. This might enable the partnership to reach the best game contract of 3NT.

Against the actual contract of four spades, West led a top diamond and then switched to the ace and another heart. The winning play is obviously to run the second heart to the jack, but the declarer was understandably frightened of losing a third-round ruff if West had started with A–x of hearts. He therefore went up with the king of hearts at trick three, hoping to discard dummy's remaining heart on a diamond if East had no entry to his presumed queen of hearts. This clever defence meant that East–West were able to cash two diamonds and two hearts to defeat the contract by one trick; without West's deceptive switch at the second trick, declarer would have been able to draw trumps and make ten tricks by way of five trump tricks, one heart, two diamonds and two clubs.

Finally, an intriguing deal from the 1983 Guardian Easter Tournament. It seems to me that West should realise that, left to his own devices, South will come to ten tricks by playing on cross ruff lines. The winning defence is therefore to switch to a trump, conceding an immediate trump trick but obtaining two tricks in return when South is compelled to change his line of play.

Dealer North; love all.

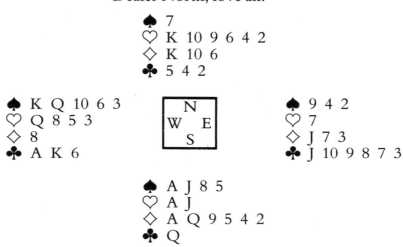

```
                    ♠ 7
                    ♡ K 10 9 6 4 2
                    ♢ K 10 6
                    ♣ 5 4 2
  ♠ K Q 10 6 3         N           ♠ 9 4 2
  ♡ Q 8 5 3          W   E         ♡ 7
  ♢ 8                  S           ♢ J 7 3
  ♣ A K 6                          ♣ J 10 9 8 7 3
                    ♠ A J 8 5
                    ♡ A J
                    ♢ A Q 9 5 4 2
                    ♣ Q
```

South	West	North	East
Mrs Flodquist		Flodquist	
		2◇(1)	NB
3◇(2)	3♠	4◇	NB
4♡(3)	Dble	NB	NB
NB			

(1) A Multi Two Diamonds, showing a weak two in either major suit or a strong balanced hand. As you will have read elsewhere in these pages, this modern convention is not among my favourites.

(2) Showing a strong hand and a good diamond suit.

(3) By now, South had a pretty fair idea what her partner's two diamond opening was based on. It seems very odd to me that she had to rely on the opponents to tell her what kind of hand her partner held.

At the table, West began with two top clubs. Mrs Flodquist ruffed the second round, crossed to dummy by ruffing a spade and ruffed dummy's last club with the ace of hearts. She then crossed to dummy with the king of diamonds and played the king and 10 of hearts, thereby restricting her losers to two trumps and one club. Plus 790 and a 'top' for the Flodquists.

Assuming that East contributes the jack of clubs at trick one, showing a solid sequence, the winning defence is for West to switch to a small trump into South's tenace. Declarer wins with the jack, ruffs a spade in dummy and ruffs a club with the ace of hearts, on which West must unblock the king of clubs.

At this point, South has to cross back to dummy in order to play on trumps. To do so by way of a second spade ruff would shorten dummy's trumps excessively and leave declarer exposed to a forcing defence. South therefore has to play a diamond to the king and play the king and 10 of hearts, but West is now in control: he wins with the queen of hearts, crosses to his partner's hand by leading his carefully-preserved small club, and collects a diamond ruff to defeat the contract by one trick.